For the Tempus-Fugitives

CRITICAL
VOICES

General Editor: David Jonathan Y. Bayot

For Val

CHRISTOPHER NORRIS

For the Tempus–Fugitives

Poems and Verse-Essays

ACADEMIC
PRESS
Brighton • Portland • Toronto

2 4 6 8 10 9 7 5 3 1

Published and distributed in the Philippines under ISBN 978-971-555-644-6 by
De La Salle University Publishing House
2401 Taft Avenue, 0922 Manila, Philippines

This edition published and distributed under ISBN 978-1-84519-867-1 in
Great Britain in 2017 by SUSSEX ACADEMIC PRESS
PO Box 139, Eastbourne BN24 9BP

and in North America by SUSSEX ACADEMIC PRESS
ISBS Publisher Services
920 NE 58th Ave #300, Portland, OR 97213

Cover Design: John David Roasa.
Cover Image: Bernie Lira.

British Library Cataloguing in Publication Data
A CIP catalogue record for this book is available from the British Library.

Library of Congress Cataloging-in-Publication Data
Norris, Christopher
For the tempus-fugitives : poems and verse-essays / Christopher Norris
   — [Manila] :
De La Salle University Publishing House, 2017.
2017 254 pages ; 23 cm. — (Critical Voices)
ISBN: 978-971-555-644-6 (pbk), in the Critical Voices series
1. English literature—History and criticism. I. Title.

Typeset & designed by De La Salle University Publishing House.

CONTENTS

Preface

I

It is not hard to find plausible reasons for the decline in popularity of the verse-essay, along with its (slightly) less formal sibling the verse-epistle, over the past century and more. The genre had its heyday in the eighteenth century among poets like Dryden, Pope, Johnson, Swift, and many nowadays less-known figures who used it to discuss all sorts of topics from politics and history to philosophy, religion, morals, literature, science, and their own day-to-day lives. This they did for the most part in rhymed and metrically regular verse with iambic pentameter very much the norm. There was also a strong preference for rhyming couplets with frequent use of end-stopping, i.e., with a more or less emphatic end-of-line metrical halt to the couplet just where the sentence or grammatical construction likewise concludes. The manner was thus highly formal, at least to present-day tastes, though in the right hands capable of great tonal, rhythmic, and stylistic variety, as will soon strike any responsive reader of a well-edited selection. Above all it was capable of doing things—arguing, reasoning, debating, controverting, reflecting on matters particular and general—in a way that very largely disappeared from English poetry with the advent of Romanticism and later movements of thought, whether post-, neo-, or (like mainstream literary modernism) officially anti-Romantic.

I think that those things are still worth doing and that it is only through tunnel-vision or the set of generic filters imposed by the Romantic-to-Modernist viewpoint that readers now tend to think of poetry—"real" poetry—as simply or properly not in that line of business. William Empson, one of its finest practitioners, coined the word *argufying* to describe what he thought of as the right way to carry this off without sacrificing vigorous argument to the requirements of disciplined yet lively versification or (just as important) the demands of verse to those of argumentative relevance or point. His own verse-practice offered the best working definition: a mode (something more than "style") of reasoning that doesn't try for anything like deductive or strict demonstrative rigor but which none the less seeks the reader's assent on broadly rational, reasonable, or common-sense terms. At the same time—and quite compatibly with that—the verse should have enough formal structure to carry on some fairly lengthy trains of thought without sagging or losing impetus while also having sufficient rhythmic variety and unexpected or striking turns of rhyme to keep the reader actively engaged. As hardly needs saying there has to be a constant interplay or tension between meter and natural speech-rhythms such that the two never perfectly coincide but set up an asynchronous counterpoint that again helps to stimulate ear and mind.

Empson managed all this to marvelous effect, though perhaps the best examples are to be found in his later, more relaxed or conversational poems. His better-known early pieces—written while still an undergraduate at Cambridge and very consciously imitating Donne—are often so intellectually taxing or wiredrawn (so "conceited," as Johnson said of the metaphysical poets) that they don't fully meet the above (albeit rough) specifications. What is crucial is that the verse should carry the argument along in a natural-sounding way while also pointing up salient details, introducing nuances of tone or implication, and sometimes (especially through inventive or unusual rhyme-words) sending thought off in a new direction that very likely wouldn't have occurred to a prose writer. This is how it works in the best eighteenth-century instances and how I have tried to make it work here, although with how much success of course only the reader can say. One thing that definitely won't work for contemporary poets or readers is that heavily end-stopped line so characteristic of Pope and Dryden when delivering some weighty generalization, drawing some sententious moral conclusion, or skewering some literary rival. To modern ears it has an insufferable air of arrogance or assumed superior wisdom, as well as an artificial elegance all too redolent of social-cultural privilege. My poems depart so far from that style as to take enjambment as the norm along with a high proportion of lengthy sentences, complex syntactic structures, multiple subordinate clauses, and a liberal use of devices—such as extended analogy—that likewise hold out against any sense of premature or forceful closure.

Giorgio Agamben has raised this—or something like it—to a high point of poetic-philosophical principle by maintaining (with reference to Dante) that poetry just is, or is most essentially, language of the kind where syntax and meter fail to coincide. So if closure, or bringing poems to an end, has often been a problem for poets it is because the final word or syllable of a poem's last line is the place where that enlivening tension, thus far sustained by enjambment, is itself of necessity brought to an end with syntax and meter more or less forcibly synchronized. I wouldn't go so far as Agamben in making their disjunction the *sine qua non* of authentic poetry and their convergence a source of inevitable crisis or breakdown. All the same I would accept the more moderate claim that such effects of formal non-synchrony or irresolution play a large role in distinguishing poetic from prose discourse. One way of looking at modernism in English poetry is to trace it back to the Romantic revolt—most vehemently expressed by Wordsworth—against "poetic diction" of the kind (especially the eighteenth-century kind) that foregrounded that distinction. From there the story goes, in very rough outline, *via* the French Symbolists (who famously thought that poetry should aspire to the condition of music and hence seek to minimize its rational-discursive and referential aspects) to arch-modernists like Pound, Eliot, and the later Yeats along with those movements in literary criticism that turned their ideas to doctrinal and pedagogical use.

Thus the modernists—albeit in their different ways—espoused a poetics of spatial form, made image and symbol the cornerstones of their aesthetic creed, and thereby managed—ironically enough—to place a maximal distance between poetry and that "ordinary language of men" that Wordsworth championed against the artifice of "poetic diction." What helps to explain this odd turn-around is, I think, the growing prevalence of an anti-formalism that started out by identifying "artifice" with one particular, historically located set of verse-conventions and then extended the veto more broadly so that it amounted to a deep suspicion of any poetry that seemed to "argufy"—to reason its way or have designs on the reader—in Empson's sense. This reactive tendency finished by creating a neo-symbolist mystique around the very conception of poetry that was shared—as Frank Kermode shrewdly remarked in his book *Romantic Image*—by Romantics and modernists, despite the markedly anti-Romantic bent of classicizing poet-critics like Eliot and Pound. These issues are raised, if obliquely, in the short poem here about Henri Matisse and the late series of cut-out colored paper-based works that were brought together in a highly acclaimed exhibition at the Tate Modern Gallery in April 2014. The epigraphs make a few relevant points concerning the aesthetics of this art-form, its relation to practical constraints imposed by the artist's advanced age and failing state of health, and the whole question of how the art-world copes with such challenges to its normative or instituted values. But in the background of the poem there is that question of the vexed though at times creatively productive relation between image and discourse, symbol and statement, picture and verbal description, or artwork (poetry included) and commentary. These are dualisms—latent polarities, even antagonisms—that seem to emerge repeatedly in my poems and no doubt convey a certain defensive edge in the face of that romantic-modernist bias toward the first term in each of the above pairs.

The epigraph from poet Fleur Adcock was included as a bit of self-irony or self-admonition on my part since she is saying that it took enormous courage for Matisse to break with every last formal convention of existing art-practice, and that this came with the kind of supreme though unassuming self-confidence that only true genius in a state of ultimate maturity can possibly bring. I'm not at all sure—defensiveness here no doubt kicking in—that getting beyond formalism is quite such a nonpareil artistic virtue, or that it has to go along with quite such a dead-set devaluation of other poetic virtues or claims on our interest like those I've been canvassing here. Besides, there is a strong formal component to the Matisse cut-outs without which their perhaps more obvious coloristic and sensuous elements would have no lasting appeal. Still the reader will have twigged by now that these poems of mine are not the productions of someone with a refined or highly developed visual-pictorial imagination. The truth is I don't get "mental pictures" of the kind most readers describe themselves as getting even when I read what are commonly taken to be vividly descriptive or visually evocative poems. No doubt this aspect of (as the current wisdom has it) left-hemisphere cerebral dominance is reflected in the character of these verse-essays with their prevailingly philosophical, argumentative, conceptual, discursive, and theoretically informed character.

If we're to go along with Roman Jakobson's bipolar taxonomy then this means that they belong very much on the metonymic as opposed to the metaphoric axis of his structural-linguistic grid. They tend to line up with such associated terms as *prose, realism, classicism, allegory, metonymic displacement,* and *documentary writing* rather than such presumptively antithetical terms as *poetry, surrealism* (or *anti-realism*), *modernism, symbol, metaphorical condensation* or *substitution*, and Barthesian *écriture*. Needless to say I don't think it works out anything like as neatly as that. Indeed I should want to make the case that my verse-essays don't so much fall short of poetry—or elect to do something altogether different—as take the alternative, predominantly metonymic path to ends or effects that, as Jakobson allows, are just as structurally complex and no less "poetic" once properly understood. There is also the point that this comparative scarcity or perceptible downplaying of devices like metaphor and symbol creates an implicit stylistic norm, and a background of readerly expectations, against which those figures stand out the more strikingly when they do turn up. It is a source of some powerful and haunting lines in poets like Auden and Larkin, so if I have brought off a similar effect on occasion then that's a not exactly unlooked-for bonus.

All of which suggests that the rejection of verse-forms such as those practiced by the eighteenth-century masters of formal prosody—or their few and most often marginalized successors—is apt in the long run to produce a poetry deficient in some of the attributes that have kept English poetry alive over the centuries. Basically they are those of formal structure and discursive or argumentative content, thought of as possessing an equal claim to good poetic standing alongside the other sorts of symbolist-formalist creed—those involving the notion of aesthetic autonomy in one or another guise—that have been more prominent over the past two centuries. So I would endorse some of Agamben's ideas about poetry—not least because they fit in rather well with my own practice here—but dissent when it comes to erecting them, as he does, into a full-scale doctrine endorsing, in effect, only poetry that satisfies his own criteria as regards the essential (poetry-constitutive) role of devices like enjambment and caesura. After all, quite simply, poems have to stop somewhere and it is far from clear that their stopping (or occasionally end-stopping) with at least a modicum of decently earned assurance is something inherently fated to compromise their distinctiveness or quality as poems. My own practice tends toward lengthy run-on constructions—encouraged (or pretty much required) by the train of thought underway—so would seem to make at least a fair shot at satisfying Agamben's formal demand. On the other hand when writing these poems, and even more when reading and revising them, I was very aware of the need to hold that tendency in check and sometimes introduce a few more places where meter and syntax conspired to offer an at any rate temporary resting-point linked to a moment of at any rate provisional stasis (or statement) in thematic-discursive terms.

II

Of course it would be absurd to reject the poetic credentials of a romantic-symbolist-modernist program that has plainly produced some magnificent poetry and done so, moreover, entirely in keeping with its own precepts. Still one may argue that when those precepts hardened—and especially when they became the basis of a full-scale program in literary criticism with doctrinal sanctions attached—then the outcome was a drastically narrowed conception of what poetry could and should achieve. What dropped out completely on that conception was the idea of it as doing some of the things that "ordinary language" does—like arguing, reasoning, putting a case, advancing a viewpoint, trying out alternative viewpoints, and so forth—but doing those things with an added cogency resulting from its various formal, structural, and stylistic attributes. Moreover it could do them without any loss of the qualities extolled by critics trained up on Eliot's idea of what constituted English poetic tradition and its high-point in the early seventeenth-century poets and verse-dramatists. For as Empson showed, in his poetry and criticism alike, those qualities—wit, paradox, verbal ingenuity, multiplied metaphor, intellectual range, the unity of thought and feeling—could perfectly well go together with a poetry that didn't shy away from rational argument or the business of actually stating a case.

It was the US New Criticism, at its academic high point in the 1950s and 60s, that took the basic tenets of literary modernism and deployed them as the basis for devising yet further methodological, doctrinal, and (ultimately) ideological restrictions on what poems—good poems—ought to be and what critics were allowed to say about them. In the latter aspect this had the effect, and purposely so, of increasing the distance between poetry and everyday discourse by erecting various rules for the conduct of good interpretative practice. They involved the orthodox New Critical veto on a number of so-called "fallacies" or "heresies," among them the recourse to authorial intention (poems were supposedly autotelic and hence quite beyond the author's power to fix their meaning just by intending it) and the appeal to biography, history, or cultural background (poems possessed meaning in and of themselves—through "the words on the page"—quite aside from such presumptively extraneous information-sources). Here again I would adduce Empson's largely neglected but utterly compelling demonstration, in *The Structure of Complex Words*, that both things can be had at once, and indeed that neither can be had in isolation. That is, a sufficiently acute close-reading will always lead us into issues of authorial intention along with biographical and socio-cultural-historical questions, while those issues and questions will always take us back—if we're to have any hope of resolving them in the only way that counts—to an ever more attentive and close-focused reading of the text.

If this is where *Complex Words* achieves a large advance over *Seven Types of Ambiguity* then it is here also that Empson breaks decisively with that whole Eliot-influenced orthodoxy according to which we cannot (or at any rate should not) mix up issues of literary interpretation with issues of intention, biography, cultural history, or—lurking behind all these—politics. For it is becoming ever clearer with hindsight just how far the academic uptake of literary modernism *via* Eliot and his disciples was shot through with political and socio-cultural value ascriptions of a highly conservative and, in some cases, deeply reactionary character. That political valence itself has much to do with the critically mediated notion of the literary work as a "verbal icon," autonomous and sufficient unto itself. In this view the poem is *a priori* unbeholden to anything that modern secularizing movements of thought might presume to extract, i.e., some message perhaps more in keeping with present-day beliefs and ideas. What Empson brings out to convincing effect is the way that such highly restrictive doctrines must perforce ignore all the most creative, inventive, and independent-minded aspects of any poetry that merits sustained close reading. Such was his answer to critics of *Seven Types*, like Rosamund Tuve, who accused him of anachronism in imputing ideas to seventeenth-century poets such as Donne and Herbert—most often skeptical counter-impulses when confronted with less than appealing aspects of Christian doctrine—as if poetry couldn't be ahead of its time or give expression to thoughts that the poet might not have consciously intended or acknowledged.

So Empson's sturdy defense of intentionalism at this stage involved some fairly large allowances for the role of unconscious or sub-doxastic ideas and beliefs. But he was later able to attack the manifest absurdity of "the Wimsatt Law"—the dogmatic anti-intentionalist case as argued most influentially by Monroe Beardsley and W. K. Wimsatt—not only on the grounds that it ignored the most basic fact about human linguistic-communicative grasp but by way of the sophisticated logico-semantic theory of interpretation advanced in *Complex Words*. His central point in all this was to defend the basic rationalist-humanist principle that the language of poetry is continuous with—and not in some prescriptive way cut off from—the language of our various non-poetic speech-acts and thought-processes. Otherwise, he thinks, we shall sell poetry short by discounting its claim on our moral, reflective, and critical intelligence while at the same time devaluing "ordinary language" by failing to appreciate the kind of creativity that goes into seemingly prosaic modes of utterance, whether of an everyday or more specialized nature. Thus he writes about those "commonplace," "flat," "unassuming" words that are apt to pass unnoticed by the guardians of ideological correctness but whose role in and effect on our thinking is all the more crucial for the fact that their semantic complexity remains well below the threshold of consciousness.

Indeed the relation between conscious and unconscious (or perhaps preconscious) components of linguistic expression is among the most complex and least understood issues in cognitive psychology and philosophy of mind, and an issue that is posed with particular force in the case of poetic language. Clearly there is much going on in poetry that exceeds or eludes the poet's conscious-intentional grasp, not least through the way that rhyme and meter interact unpredictably with what they might have in mind by way of preconceived expressive or thematic gist. Yet there is another, more encompassing, less Cartesian way of approaching the issue according to which what counts as intentional should take in mental events or contents that occur outside the spot-lit zone of punctual, self-present apperception. Taking the term in this expanded sense—as applied to thought-processes, intentions, and meanings that may be subject to a certain degree of temporal spread as well as extension beyond that overly privileged zone—makes a lot more sense in terms of how poets tend to think about the activity of composition. Here I am going partly by my own experience but also by accounts in a similar vein essayed by those for whom the writing of poetry involves a hard-to-explain combination of utterly focused—in the strictest sense "intentional"—mental states combined with an uncommon openness to sundry phonetic, semantic, and grammatical effects that seem to take on a generative power largely apart from—even against—authorial design. Poetry might even provide a useful way of thinking about issues like the problem allegedly posed to any upholder of human freewill by MRI-scan results purporting to show that brain-events occur an appreciable time before experimental subjects register their choice or conscious intent to perform some particular action. This is because poetry most strikingly exemplifies how very hard it is—and perhaps how misconceived the effort—to specify just where the line falls between conscious and unconscious/preconscious modes of thinking, willing, or intending.

III

These are some of the reasons—quite apart from the sheer challenge and satisfaction of writing in metrical, rhymed, and (for the most part) long-run narrative and argumentative forms—for my choosing to buck so many of the trends that characterize present-day poetry. The topics of my verse-essays range from the polemical to the reflective, from politics to philosophy, from the broadly general to the (relatively) personal, and from news items chosen for their comic, tragic, or socially symptomatic import to speculative themes focused on aspects of language, consciousness, or selfhood. The forms deployed are all, as I have said, highly traditional and include *terza rima*, sestinas, modified sonnet-forms, quatrains rhyming abab or abba, extensions of those basic quatrain-forms into longer (8- or 16-line) stanzas, and poems that use just two rhyme-sounds over a lengthy AB sequence with the object of sustaining interest (or avoiding boredom) through out-of-the-way rhymes that bring a

xvii

novel slant to the topic in hand. The diction is mostly of a middling character—neither highly formal nor downright demotic—though the latter does make an occasional appearance, either for contrastive effect or to express the sorts of sentiment that would come across as straight satire if couched in something closer to the formal norm established elsewhere.

Most of the poems have some kind of epigraph, quotation, headnote, or explanatory gloss supplied as a courtesy to the reader. The whole business of providing notes is a bit of a minefield, especially since Eliot filled out the blank octavo pages of the first edition of *The Waste Land* with a mass of detailed notes whose relevance or usefulness was, in many cases, open to doubt. Still Empson, as usual, offers the best case for the defense when he says that it is more considerate not to send the reader off on a time-consuming search for obscure sources of information if you have them on hand. Besides, what that reader chiefly needs to grasp if they want to understand and appreciate the poem—rather than merely know about its sources—is the process of thought whereby those sources were taken up into the author's expressive-argumentative intent, or utilized (maybe shrewdly exploited) so as to do something new and remarkable with them. As usual Empson makes all the main points in the shortest space:

> When I am not actually faced with explaining [the poems] I feel notes aren't wanted; but I think people would be more easily tempted to read verse if there was plenty of critical writing thrown in, demanding less concentration of attention, and with more literary-critical magazine or novel-reading interest—I know *I* should. And there is a rather portentous air about compact verses without notes, like a seduction without conversation.[1]

Not so "compact," the reader may remark, in the case of my own verse-essays, but the issue about notes is much the same: why not offer help where needed or desirable? So I have not let symbolist scruples or New Critical anathemas veto the provision of topical leads, pertinent items of background information, or (occasionally) suggestions as to how things fit together.

The underlying point here is Empson's continuity-principle and the fact that, theory aside, we make sense of poetry with the same range of linguistic, interpretative, pragmatic, experiential, and other such widely shared resources as we bring to bear in everyday-communicative contexts. These poems are basically speech-acts that function in various ways—argumentative, informative, persuasive, combative, reflective, suggestive, commemorative, etc.—and therefore come out strongly against any creed that denies poetry's practical-performative power in the name of aesthetic autonomy. So the epigraphs and other such (as Derrida would say) "parergonal" items are there more as semi-detachable parts of the poems than afterthoughts inserted just as a sop to those who might otherwise complain about willful or needless obscurity. Still I have not provided notes and references for the various items mentioned above since this is, after all, primarily a book of poems rather than an academic treatise. A Google search will track down almost anything nowadays with minimal effort and maximal information yield so the whole business of detailed source-referencing has become to a large extent redundant.

That Eliot's notes were such an odd mixture of useful leads and archly irrelevant pseudo-information is itself a clear sign of the modernist-mediated symbolist influence that fixes a prescriptive gulf between poetry and other kinds of discourse. No doubt this also had a lot to do with his troubled emotional life at the time of *The Waste Land*'s composition and with Eliot's desire to put critics off the biographical trail or discourage speculation about sources nearer home than many of those distractingly adduced in the notes. But it was also an outcome of that whole anti-rationalist complex of ideas that made the discontinuity between poetic and non-poetic language into a shibboleth of aesthetic, ethical, and (though rarely advertised as such) socio-political principle. If the pieces collected here go directly against that doctrine then their collective point, as distinct from other more specific intentions, is to make the case for a poetry continuous with the sorts of thinking that typically occur when people argue and exchange ideas in real-world communicative contexts. For these are situations where, as Aristotle sensibly held, rhetoric and the arts of persuasive discourse may very often count—even count crucially—without the least compromise to appropriate standards of rationality and truth. The poems are thus meant to serve as an antidote to high modernism while also signalling allegiance to that other tradition with its alternative (mainly eighteenth-century) sources and its continuation in poets of otherwise varied character like Auden, Empson, Thom Gunn, James Fenton, Tony Harrison, A.D. Hope, Louis MacNeice, Peter Porter, and (since formal excellence doesn't always go along with the ethical, political, or basic human virtues) Philip Larkin.

I should like to thank everyone who read these poems, discussed them, invited me to read them at conferences and other events, offered much-needed support and encouragement along the way, and generally helped me to feel that the project wasn't too perverse or misguided. They really are too many to mention individually and will in any case know how indebted I am so just let me mention two great singing groups, Cor Cochion Caerdydd and The Eclectics, along with my wonderfully expert, supportive, and inspirational editor David Jonathan Bayot, without whose encouragement at every stage this project would never have been carried through.

Swansea, September 2016

NOTE

1 William Empson, "Letter to Ian Parsons," cited by John Haffenden in his Introduction to Empson, *The Complete Poems*, ed. Haffenden (London: Allen Lane, 2000), p. xlviii.

Acknowledgments

Some of these poems have been published in journals or on websites as follows: *The European English Messenger*, *Journal of Humanistic Mathematics*, *RARA*, *The Recusant*, *Scintilla*, *The Seventh Quarry*, *Shakespeare Studies*, and *Think*. I am grateful to the editors and publishers concerned for their permission to reprint those pieces here, mostly in revised or modified form.

FOR THE TEMPUS-FUGITIVES

This poem has to do with a neat and arithmetically quite simple explanation of why time seems to pass more quickly as we get older, but also with the reasons why it fails to work as a matter of phenomenological (not to mention personal and emotional) conviction. That the strictures of the rhyme-scheme are meant to drive this point home the more forcefully will I hope come across as one piece of supporting evidence for my case about the merits of a formalist poetic. The title is taken from a treatise by Sextus Empiricus, the ancient skeptic, who denied that human beings were capable of attaining any kind of genuine (objective or indubitable) knowledge, mathematics being one of his case studies. My use of it implies not agreement with his views or those of his numerous latter-day progeny—indeed I have argued vigorously against them elsewhere—but rather a sense of how such skepticism chimes with the reaction of almost everyone on first encountering the math-based account of that speeding-up illusion as the body clock ages.

It stands to reason once you've got the gist
    And figured why, as life goes on, its rate
Of passage speeds up and it seems you missed
    Some annual fixture just because the date
Came round so quickly that the old check-list
    Of jobs to do or days to celebrate
At last proved quite unable to assist
    In your attempt to stop things running late.

The answer's one our number-theorist
    Has got off pat: the ratios dictate

That an inverse proportion must exist
    Between the sum of years you've had to wait
From birth till now and the contractile tryst
    Of time with life that sets life's quickening gait
From now on. Hence the chronotropic twist
    That thwarts all vain attempts to correlate

Your own time-consciousness with what they say,
    Those back-to-Newton clock-watch types who think
Its flow's so smooth and equable that they
    Can accurately gauge from link to link
Its chronometric rate. A simpler way
    Of putting it's the fact that time-scales shrink
(It seems) in keeping with the day-to-day
    Expanding ratios now required to sync

Time further-back with time not so passé
    Or time right now. This feels too like the brink
Of some catastrophe you'd kept at bay,
    If not by ministry of drugs or drink,
Then by some trick of thought that might defray
    The cost by making out that there's a chink
In that proportion-scheme so things obey
    Sir Isaac's second law and, in a blink,

Accelerate so fast you'll never know
    What happened in the end. So they compute
Quite logically, those speed-ups in the flow
    Of human time whose rate turns out to suit
The number-crunchers who purport to show
    How everything's numerical at root,
Or how those mid-to-late-life crises go
    Directly into mathemes that commute

Life-sentences to short-term. These bestow
　　The Pythagorean leisure to impute
All such small upsets to the quid pro quo
　　Of time and number that the more astute
Or numerate among us reckon no
　　Great cause for mental anguish so acute
Since merely products of a ratio
　　Whose shortening odds no life-hope could refute.

Yet it's through just their method to explain
　　That hope's eclipse (they say) that we may find
More adequate resources to maintain
　　Some equipoise once sensibly resigned
To overtaking in an outside lane
　　Marked "Pile-Up Just Ahead," while way behind
There fades from view our last hope to regain
　　That old co-temporality of mind

And world inhabiting the one domain
　　Of a life-time that let them both unwind
Without such contretemps. If we refrain
　　From all vain efforts later on to bind
The time-scales so they synchronize again,
　　Or do the sums until we're disinclined
To find a cause of existential pain
　　In functions mathematically defined,

Then (they propose) we'll emulate the best
　　Of Pascal's thinking. These are not the bits
About how small he felt or how depressed
　　By sheer immensities or infinites,
But more the thought-experiments that test
　　Just how those intuitions fare when it's

A matter for math-specialists possessed
　　Of some technique that more exactly fits

Our need to steer well clear of such distressed
　　Mind-zones and so make sure the thing submits
To problem-solving powers beyond what messed
　　With Pascal's *autre soi*. Thus it permits
(They'd have us think) the well-schooled mind to wrest
　　Some glimpse of truth and order from the pits
Of inchoate emotion that expressed
　　No more than our desire to call it quits

With time's fast-forward. Granted, they've a fair
　　Entitlement, those thinkers, to proclaim
By dint of proof demonstrative that their
　　Procedure's what best justifies the name
Of truth and best equips us to prepare
　　For moves in the timescale-adjustment game
Since otherwise the mounting odds would scare
　　Us half to death. Then we'd be prone to blame

The very thought-techniques that did their share
　　To quiet our fears for putting us to shame
By showing how we lacked the strength to bear
　　Such undeluding truths. Yet, if we came
Up against some *mémoire involontaire*,
　　Perhaps some near-death flashback that could frame
And shrink our lifetime to an instant where
　　The ratios went sky-high, then all the same,

Despite our having taken full on board
　　All that the *mathematikoi* had taught

Our time-sick souls, their cure might not afford
    Us mental strength enough to face the sort
Of panic-state that used to have us floored
    And does right now. Then we perceive how short
Such mind-games fall of finding some accord
    Between that old, inconsolable thought

Of *temps* too soon *perdu* and tricks that scored
    Top points for puzzle-solving though they brought
No sense of *kairos* gratefully restored
    Or gift to heal the damage *chronos* wrought
When clock-time calibrated. This ignored
    Its finely gauged potential to distort
Whatever our life-histories have shored
    Against time's shrewd contrivances to thwart

The time-shaped craving that time should reward
    Us tempus-fugitives with times less fraught
Since amply sutured by the triple cord
    Of body, mind and world that time holds taut.

DIABOLUS IN MUSICA

> *Legend has it that an 11th century Benedictine monk and vocal tutor Guido d'Arezzo coined the dictum "mi contra fa est diabolus in musica" ("Mi with Fa is the devil in music") to discourage vocalists from using specific dissonant intervals...Here are the implied "mi–fa" combinations including inversions: C to B is a 7th. F to B is a #4th. B to C is a 2nd. B to F is a ♭5th. Curiously it is only the ♭5th of these intervals that retains the demonic moniker in modern times.*

> —Guy Pople

> *There are strict musical rules. You aren't allowed to use this particular dissonance. It simply won't work technically, you are taught not to write that interval. But you can read into that a theological ban in the guise of a technical ban.*

> —John Deathridge

I

Diabolus in musica: they feared
   The tritone like the devil; how its spell
Wrought discord in the souls of listeners reared

In diatonic ways and conjured hell-
   On-earth to those few auditors sharp-eared
Enough to catch what tales it had to tell

Of chaos come again. As music veered
　　About the octave's midpoint so the well-
Trained contrapuntalists who'd once adhered

To Rome's strict rule were driven to rebel,
　　Junk all the compass-points by which they'd steered
Well clear of rocks so far, and thenceforth dwell

Way out beyond the tonal safe-zone cleared
　　By guardians of the faith. And so it fell
On their shocked sense as if the devil jeered

At every effort to suppress or quell
　　The restlessness that surfaced in such weird
Though ear-beguiling sounds as might compel,

Alas, such devilish deafness to revered
　　And hallowed teachings.

II

　　　　　　　Forward wind: Purcell
Writes harmonies that, for the Fathers, seared

The listener's soul but makes the most of their
　　Now devil-free potential to augment
Both simple fourths and whatsoever share

Of grief those intervals might represent,
　　Yet in a way that bids the church forebear
To challenge or proscribe since clearly meant

To signal how its dissonance may square
    With what fresh scope the Reformation lent
To such displays of feeling. These declare

How all the major–minor shifts that went,
    Back then, to plant the warning sign "Beware,
Forbidden territory" now circumvent

That rule by saying: hear the soul at prayer
    In harmonies that speak of its intent
To cast aside all rules that might impair

True passion's voice. How else should it lament,
    As Purcell did, when called upon to spare
No depth of feeling such as once he'd spent

Great effort to suppress but now took care,
    As in his Funeral Sentences, to vent
In ways that few before or since would dare.

III

Sibelius Four: the tritones occupy
    Almost the whole of tonal space, yet stay
Well short of atonality. For why

Take Schoenberg's route and leave yourself no way
    To raise the norm of dissonance so high
Within that space that music might convey

Such harsh and hard-won truths? They fructify,
  Those tritones, till the only truths that they
Afford the listener willing to get by

On such cold comfort rests in what they say
  Of how the laws of entropy apply
To music, how the living sounds decay,

How vainly the negentropists deny
  What no mere shift of key can long delay,
Or how those demon intervals they try

Through careful filtering to hold at bay
  Must shortly find them out and so defy
Their sanguine gloss. If seasoned listeners pay

The devil his due it's when keys go awry,
  When some chord-sequence instantly falls prey
To ear's equivalent of evil-eye

And false relations once again betray
  The tritone's devilry. So all hopes die
Of any modulation fit to play

A saving role and reassert the tie
  Of tonic-dominant that kept such stray
Augmented intervals from letting fly

With aural weaponry designed to fray
  Those homely chords. Yet still the tritones vie
For extra *Lebensraum*, strive as we may

To tune out alien frequencies, decry
   Their every land-grab, and resist the sway
Of alien powers. That's why our ears fight shy

Each time that E flat modulates to A.

WEATHER

'Weather forecast for tonight: dark.' (George Carlin)

The night before, quite late, was when you said
   How other people change in just the way
The weather changes; how we plan ahead,

Switch plans with what the latest forecasts say,
   And tend to take it pretty much as read
They'll not be too far out. Yet, come the day,

Us trusting types may find we've been misled
   By the same over-confidence that they,
The weather-experts, showed. Let's think instead

(You mused that night as nerves began to fray
   And time drew on but still not time for bed)
That what sends all those best-laid plans astray

Is what the wisest people-watchers dread
   As much as weather-watchers. Our dismay
When things go wrong then tells us we must shed

The old delusion that we knew what lay
   Days, hours or minutes off and learn to tread
More cautiously so as to keep at bay

The kinds of future-shock designed to shred
  Our puny storm-defences. If we play
Along with the old forecast-game that spread

Such confidence it's odds-on we'll betray,
  Like me next day, the false assurance bred
By seasonal routines that first convey

Glad tidings but, when once we lose the thread
  And panic strikes, collapse the whole array
Of habit-formed expectances that fed

Our need to buck the odds and disobey
  The canny gambler's rule. If I saw red
That morning or put up some fool display

Of teacup storm-cloud conjuring that led
  To an occluded cold front, one that may
Prefigure climate-change, then what you said

The previous night, though true, is apt to prey
  More harshly on mild weather-watchers wed,
Like me, to forecasts saying things will stay

Much as they were till all the lines go dead.

LOST SOULS

Dear Dr. Weeks,
I would think that as people get older their eccentricities would become more evident as they would be more able to express themselves freely. Instead I find the opposite. Most senior citizens are total conformists who don't want to deviate from the pack in any way. Are my observations valid? Do tendencies to express yourself change with age?
—Carol

Dear Carol,
Generally speaking, eccentric people become more eccentric with age. However, eccentric people do not become eccentric in old age; most eccentrics become eccentric in childhood or adolescence. If a person, especially a male, were first to show eccentric behavior in old age, as a clinician I would consider other causes. It would suggest illness, either of a psychiatric or physical nature. However, where there are higher concentrations of older retired people—in Britain, around the seacoast—there will be more older eccentric people, perhaps because eccentrics tend to live longer.

Yours sincerely,
Dr. David Weeks

Time was when university or church
    Offered a bolt-hole, refuge in distress,
Or last-chance hideaway for those in search

Of any spot where their contrariness,
    Their stubborn eccentricity or lack
Of *savoir-faire* might not make such a mess

Of things or let catastrophes so stack
    Up that they'd more than likely come to grief
Should circumstance decree they venture back

Into the outside world. There's no relief
    Now for these émigrés to inner space
Except the dubious blessing of a brief

And youthful intermission at some place
    Of "higher learning" where the main idea
Is higher earning, or—as in the case

Of those for whom the other-worldly sphere
    Is theocentric—some sequestered school
Of faith and ministry. Whence they'll appear,

Some few years on, to play the holy fool,
    Though scarcely blessed with what Erasmus thought
The higher wisdom that, by a strict rule

Of role-reversal, was most aptly taught
    By those accounted fools on any score
Drawn up by all the wise guys. Now they're caught,

Imperfect fools, without the old rapport
    That put them on a wavelength finely tuned
To God's own channel so that they implore

Our charitable alms like souls marooned
    By backwash from the "melancholy, low,
Withdrawing roar" to which the lovers swooned

In Arnold's loss-of-faith seduction show.
   Now the mudflat-revealing tidal reach
Just goes to show how far that long-ago

Consolatory scene on Dover Beach
   Falls short of any promise to console
These scholar-gypsies of our time, or teach

Them an updated version of the role
   In which he neatly managed to combine
Those low-prophetic vibes (sea over shoal,

Love over waning faith) with a good line
   In classy chat-up talk. Not so his lost
Inheritors whom fate or genes consign

To mere perdition as the hidden cost
   Our modernizers one and all see fit
To pay while little heeding who gets tossed

Into the limbo of stray souls that flit
   Disconsolate from worldly scene to scene
Until they either find the nerve to quit

That whole charade or take the might-have-been
   Replacement world of make-believe as their
Safe haven from the pressures of routine

Or fears of how the actual may ensnare
   The possible. At any rate no scope
For those who'd draw a *cordon sanitaire*

Around their eccentricity and hope
    By that to keep the new regime at bay,
Or give themselves a bit of room to cope

With the new rule-book drawn up to convey
    A blunt demand. This says they'd better stick
Within the bounds of *actualité*

And do their level-headed best to kick
    Those self-indulgent reveries that grant
Them absolution simply at the flick

Of a switch wired to make it seem they can't,
    For now at least, be subject to the kinds
Of norm that rule no fiction should supplant

The *hic et nunc* of more resilient minds.
    And then, as if such chivvying weren't enough
To fray the nerves of anyone who finds

No comfort-zone in that quotidian stuff
    But ample cause for fear, there's what they've done,
Those new viceroys of academe, to snuff

Out the last sparks of selfhood, one by one,
    And so at last inaugurate the reign
Of universal dullness. This might run

As if in grooves so long as they remain
    Sole arbiters of what should make the grade
As four-star scholarship and what they deign

To mention, if at all, under some trade-
    Description such as "Miscellaneous," "Type
Four: other public output," or just "Weighed

In our research-grant scales and rated tripe
    By all the indicators." Then, worse still,
There's the unspoken flipside of this hype

For rule-bound mediocrity that will,
    Once prompted, find occasion to suggest
That, sad to say, they're way over the hill,

Those name-antiquities, or past their best
    In terms of anything that might compute
With management or pass the final test

Of excellence requiring that one suit
    One's own objectives to the standard set
By corporate bosses eager to recruit

Young talent bright and keen enough to get
    A toehold on the ladder, although not
So bright and keen as might just pose a threat

To corporate values. As a parting shot
    Line-managers can nowadays inject
That weasel-word, "eccentric," that they jot

Down once the tick-box bits have all been checked,
    With a strong hint that here the word implies
Not "pretty crazy, as you might expect

Of one so highly gifted," nor "defies
    Our best attempts to place them on a scale
Drawn up for lesser minds," but—in the guise

Of fond indulgence—more a bid to nail
    Their "eccentricity" as bearing all
The tell-tale marks of intellect grown frail,

Or mind that's frankly not quite on the ball
    And needs a rest. Behind it looms the great
New terror whose first tell-tale signs appall

The self-observer whose declining state
    Becomes the single focus of their own
And others' urgent need to estimate

What's left of mind or selfhood in that zone
    Of indistinction where their power to bring
About Kant's fragile bond of knower and known

Grows weaker as they desperately cling
    To its last vestiges. This cruelest twist
Of implication is the very thing

Most needed by the canny strategist
    One of whose tasks is quietly to propose
A means by which some colleagues might be kissed

Goodbye with no requirement to disclose
    Good grounds or reason since it's pretty much
The common wisdom now that most of those

Past middling years will likely show a touch
　　Of (let's say) idiosyncrasy. And then,
More senior still—once they've advanced to such

An age as tops the old three-score-and-ten—
　　They start to recognise the shifty look
And awkward topic-change that follows when

They talk about the article or book
　　They're working on, or how they're keen to take
A term's research-leave (since the last they took

Was decades back), if only for the sake
　　Of catching up with all the latest trends
Or struggling, for the umpteenth time, to make

Some sense of deconstruction. Even friends,
　　They've noticed, seem increasingly to shy
Away when some chance conversation tends

Toward topics that might prompt the question why
　　Their work's not featured anywhere among
The departmental listings, or—to try

Their patience further—why slips of the tongue,
　　Like "Prof. Emeritus," so often turn
Up just when some research committee's sprung

The kind of news they're always last to learn,
　　Though always first to suffer from through cuts
In funding. Hence those motions to adjourn

Decision-making till the ifs and buts
　　Can be thrashed out by colleagues with a due
Sense of the risk that their department shuts

For want of room to move them up the queue,
　　Those bright young scholars fresh from Ph.D.'s
On the right topics and keen to pursue

Careers best suited to their expertise.
　　In short, the system's jammed if all the roads
That lead to academe are blocked from these

Exemplary observers of the codes
　　And protocols by a large rump of old
Retainers hanging on in sheer busloads

Until kicked out, or dead, or firmly told
　　To step aside. Else they're kept on in some
Near-sinecure that feels like they're paroled,

Not as with those let out though told to come
　　Back punctually but those allowed to hang
Around on strict condition they'll keep mum

And spare their colleagues all that *Sturm und Drang*
　　Self-pitying stuff when finally it's time
For new blood to invigorate the gang

While they bow out content with the sublime
　　Self-abnegating ruse of saying they've
Been hoping all along the thing would chime

With their plans for retirement. Yet to stave
   It off like that, the death-watch count that starts
With gifts and talk of service that they gave

For such long years, may very well touch hearts,
   Their own included, for a while but soon
Gives way to the hard lesson it imparts

That their departure's nothing but a boon
   To those well-wishers. And it turns out just
The same with everything they'd thought immune

To time's long-term revenges, from the trust
   They'd placed in higher learning to the worth
Of some few books and articles that must,

They'd thought, do something to make up the dearth
   Of other things by which—since it's the sort
Of wish we're apt to have—their stay on earth

Should stay in mind. Thus people might report.
   How their old colleague, now retired, had "left
This world a better place," or not been short

Of kind words for the suffering or bereft,
   Or—in their case a somewhat smaller stretch
Of counterfactual thinking—shown a deft

And tactful touch in knowing how to fetch
   Up ego-soothing ways to heal a rift
Between old colleagues. But if that's the sketch

They like to draw as summing up the drift
　　Of their own *Times* obituary this fond
Self-image proves apt to get shorter shrift

With each hard knock against the world beyond
　　Their donnish fantasy. For now it's past
Reviving like some far-back *autre monde,*

That time when colleges retained a cast
　　Of amiable eccentrics whose chief claim
To any good repute that might outlast

Their tenure or afford them local fame
　　Was down to such remembrance plus a bunch
Of minor publications to their name

If so desired. But then there came the crunch,
　　The new *Gleichschaltung* under which regime
The old dissenters were ruled out to lunch

And those with all the power in academe,
　　Mid-managers and up, took special pains
To stress how everybody on the team

Must show not merely that they had the brains
　　But that they'd seen right through the old pretence
Which says: there's only one thing that explains

How genius outperforms intelligence
　　And that's (as Pope described it) something "sure
To madness near allied" where plain-prose sense

Recedes from view. A self-applied quick cure
	For such ideas is what the times require
And what best helps the new lot reassure

Their research-managers that they aspire
	No higher than to make that mid-life switch
To management themselves, and then retire

After a smooth career-path without hitch
	Since perfectly adjusted to the need
That all who take it be prepared to ditch

Such rogue ambitions. These were what decreed
	They strive above all else to leave a mark
Of individual genius or succeed

In making sure theirs is the only spark
	Of intellectual brilliance that shines out
As one fixed beacon in the deepest dark

Whose signal power such individuals tout
	Against the heaviest odds. If these are stacked
Too high to leave the outcome in much doubt

Then put it down to the implicit pact
	Between those fixers of a fine new deal
For management and all the shifts it tracked

In public mood, like how the old appeal
	Of 'eccentricity' and all those tales
Of absent-minded profs have come to feel

Distasteful now that everybody quails
  Before the prospect of their own last years,
Or how it goes as each last system fails

And there's no way to calm the mounting fears
  With Einstein-anecdotes that used to hike
The spirits but now seem a myth that cheers

Only the credulous. Yet, lest it strike
  The mind-administrators as a piece
Of crass pop-science conjured up to spike

Their bureaucratic guns or mere caprice
  Of tenured scatter-wits, let this thought cross
Their own much tidier minds: should that lot cease

Their errant ways then how compute the loss?

A WORD CHILD

Certain cerebrovascular disasters are called "insults to the brain"…the more prodigious the brain, the more studious (and in this case protracted) the insult. Iris's brain was indeed prodigious.

Soon, "the most intelligent woman in England" (Bayley's plausible evaluation) is watching the Teletubbies with a look of awed concentration on her face.

—Martin Amis, The Guardian, *December 21, 2001*

CBeebies helps; the Teletubbies tell
   Nice stories with no need for stuff about
Despair, life-crises, *Angst*, ideas that "hell
   Is other people," existential doubt,

Or authenticity. Time was, she'd dwell,
   She and her characters, on ways to tout
Love-interests of the sort that went down well
   With readers chiefly keen to figure out

What latest *crise de conscience* might compel
   Some new twist in the story-line or bout
Of agonised soul-searching. Now the spell
   Cast on her by this glossolalic rout

Of tiddler-tv dummies works to quell
  Her rare face-clouding intervals of doubt
When voices from beyond the painted shell
  Of wonder-land might just be heard to shout

The curse that once resounded from the bell
  In her most gothic novel, yet without
Its old power to appal. For now they fell
  From far off on the ears of one devout

No longer in response to its dark knell
  But to how Laa-Laa, Po and Dipsy flout
All rules of sense by which their clientele
  Of infant viewers might be caused to pout.

A FAMILY BUSINESS

"A Family Business" has to do with Margaret Thatcher's chapel-going childhood, her small-town petty-bourgeois social background, her rise to power, her domestic and foreign policies, and above all the massive and enduring effects of her period in office. The poem will I think be fairly uncontroversial in reflecting on her father's likely influence but perhaps more of a red rag to various bulls in what it says about the tenacity, psychological depth, and morally damaging character of that influence. There are moments of comparative light relief but the piece is basically an exercise in Juvenalian *saeva indignatio*, or the sort of satire that takes no hostages and which extends no tolerant ironic allowances for human frailty or untoward circumstance. In fact there are passages where the *indignatio* almost overwhelms the satire and, as tends to happen with such writing, the poetry takes on a decidedly angry—though I hope not abrasive—tone.

Three pews back on the right she sits, devout
    And hanging on each word the preacher aims
At those few souls elect who know about

Shop-keeping and the providential claims
    Of shrewd accountancy along with that
Fine double-entry scheme of things that frames

Their godly warrant for arriving at
    New ways to optimise the current state
Of family fortunes. This they've got off pat

Through years of diligence to correlate
    Their Christian faith with what attracts the most
Lucrative custom at the lowest rate

Of overheads or taxes one could boast
    About in decent company and not
Raise pious eyebrows. There she sits, engrossed,

As he (her father) tells them how they've got
    To lay up worldly goods as well as store
Up blessings that would pay out on the dot

At that great day of reckoning when the more
    Astute among them who'd resolved to look
Out for themselves and theirs would surely score

Top marks in God's panoptic ledger-book
    Of souls redeemed. Not so that other bunch
Whose talk of social conscience showed they took

The gospel texts to preach some out-to-lunch,
    Most likely socialist idea of how
To save us from the moral credit-crunch

That came of living for the here-and-now
    Of private greed. On this he reassured
His restive congregation: they allow,

Indeed demand, a gloss for readers cured
    Of such delusive notions and aware
That what most efficaciously ensured

The soul's deliverance from its mortal share
   Of sinfulness was not the vain desire
To give up, Lear-like, all the goods in their

Hard-won possession. Let them heed the prior
   Since commerce-tested maxim that the way
To true salvation might instead require

That one give up those hopelessly *passé*
   Ideas of soul-salvation that decreed
An end to acquisition and convey,

Rather, the soul's as well as body's need
   For laying in enough to see them through
Hard times ahead. Then maybe they'd succeed

(The alderman admonished) and undo
   The ill effects of that false message spread
By liberals and social-hopers who

Believed the task of giving daily bread
   To those in need of it was higher on
The to-do list than seeking to embed

The fear of God in human hearts far gone
   In wickedness. His daughter ponders this
And other points in his distinctly non-

PC approach that some might take amiss
   Though just the cure (she thinks) for that malaise
Of faith misplaced that looks for future bliss

In some fine programme for a higher phase
   Of ethical advancement when the whole
Existing scheme will enter its last days

And then emerge transformed. She sees her role
   Already as the messenger who'll bear
His tidings from that chapel where the sole

Mark of success was rousing folk to prayer
   And make of it a doctrine that would cause
Even old socialists, caught unaware

By her new gospel-truth, to doubt the laws
   Of progress. These (they took it) should consist
In keeping their utopias on pause,

Projecting justice as a long-term tryst
   With history, and—when medium-term defeats
Piled up—recalling all the chances missed

As evidence of how the world mistreats
   Those visionary few who'd prove at last
The ones who got it right. In the mean streets

Of Grantham, Lincs, the *Zeitgeist* stands aghast
   As those beliefs that once maintained a bond
Between politicos of every cast

From centre-left to centre-right, beyond
   Mere party politics, are felt to lose
All pertinence and so at length respond

By self-destructing as the parties choose
    Their lesser evil or, more often, opt
For some malign amalgam that would fuse

The worst of every world. Why had they stopped,
    She wondered, those old Tories she despised,
Short of the perfect answer: to adopt

The techniques he'd successfully devised,
    Her preacher-patriarch, to keep his flock
Of listeners so routinely unsurprised,

Like her, by such hard sayings as would shock
    Those with more tender consciences, upset
The 'Socialists for Jesus' lot, or knock

A hole in all things shored against the threat
    Of old Jehovah. These might take the form
Of biblical remonstrance or be let

Loose like a kind of Benjaminian storm
    From paradise that left its mounting pile
Of debris and propelled the shambling swarm

Of progress-touters forward all the while
    Toward the same catastrophe whose dread
Event he'd conjured up. His graphic style

Left little doubt of how it should be read
    By God's elect as yet another sign,
If such were needed, that the daily bread

The Lord's Prayer spoke of, like the loaves and wine
  Of Canaan, figured forth the moral good
Of gainful trade. Let no-one then repine,

He cautioned, if the texts thus understood
  Seemed lacking in those qualities that earned
The praise of social-gospellers who could,

By cunning tweaks, convince us they discerned
  In scripture Christ's intention to inspire
His followers, then and now, with lessons learned

From proto-communism's book, or fire
  Their fervent souls with some perverse new take
On the old texts that reckoned all their dire

Apocalyptic prophecies would make,
  If suitably construed, a fine device
To turn his message right around and shake

Its biblical foundations. So they'd splice,
  Those heretics, a secularizing mode
Of exegesis with the kind of twice-

Born zeal for some redemptive twist that showed
  Them destined from the outset to that fate
Decreed for all who falsified the code

Of scripture since they thought such change of state
  Pertained to Caesar's realm or the domain
Of social justice where we might create

Some ersatz heaven on earth. This he'd explain
    By citing verse and chapter week by week
Until his exhortations filled her brain

With their bewildering mix of bible-speak
    And his own trademark brand of *Poujadiste*
Small-town *ressentiment* that made him seek,

Each Sunday, some occult sign of the beast
    Now slouching close. Or he'd find nearer home
Some new and shocking sign of how we'd ceased

To honour parents, dutifully comb
    The Good Book for instruction, hold in awe
The Ten Commandments, count the Church of Rome

Most grievously in breach of every law
    Laid down for our salvation, and—his theme
In stressful times—acknowledge the deep flaw

In human nature. This should make it seem
    Sheer hubris, so the lesson ran, to think
In terms of social progress or to deem

Us capable of virtues that would prink
    Our defects out in any decent dress
That wouldn't, on a closer viewing, shrink

Down in the undeceiving wash to stress
    How chronically deluded were those folk
Who pinned our only chance of blessedness

To hopes like these. The truth of what he spoke
    She came to think self-evident, and so
Considered it her greatest master-stroke

In later times of crisis to forego
    All queasy conscience-searching and endorse
That same bone-deep and chapel-nurtured low

Opinion of mankind that had its source,
    Not only in his fixed idea of sin
Congenital and passed down through the course

Of post-Edenic history, but in
    His having cautioned her to disregard
All claims that "social progress" let her win

Against old prejudices that died hard
    Amongst their kind. This was the sort of tale,
He said, in which those progress-mongers starred

As heroes of an exploit doomed to fail
    Since based on an agenda that proposed
Some secular deliverance from the vale

Of suffering whose significance he glozed,
    Each Sunday, as God-sanctioned to remind
The faithful of that crookedness disclosed

In the sin-darkened heart of humankind.
    Such was the message borne by gospel text
And by the clinching evidence we find

From one historic instance to the next
    Of promised heavens-on-earth that soon revealed
The age-old bitter truth whose import vexed

The social hopers since its only yield
    For them was flat despair. She had no thought
That perhaps Alfred's's take on things concealed

Motives or interests of another sort,
    That maybe his high praise for those who laid
Up earthly riches might find scant support

In holy writ, or that his daily trade
    In groceries and far from generous view
Of average human nature as displayed

In everyday transactions gives a clue
    To why his gloss on scripture took a slant
So sin-obsessed, so resolute to do

His fellow-mortals down, and keen to grant
    The ultimate depravity of all
Those secular redemptions that supplant

The progress-shattering truth. That's why they fall
    Under proscription as the devil's work
Which still (his constant theme) holds us in thrall

To heretic conclusions that can lurk
    Unnoticed in the noblest hopes and dreams
Of liberals or those whose bright-side quirk

Was liable to bring their splendid schemes
    Of social justice to the sorry end
Reserved for infidels. On suchlike themes,

With sundry variations, she'd depend
    In times to come when moral or humane
Considerations turned out to commend

Some policy that went against the grain
    Of pure self-interest, or that said we'd best
Seek public goods beyond what served to gain

The moral high ground only by the test
    Of how far public feeling might be swung
To further private ends at the behest

Of corporate interests. They ensured a bung
    By large donations at a timely stage
In her ascent to power, like those among

Her media moguls who'd been quick to gauge
    The turning tide and just as quick to seize
Their chance of giving her the full front-page

Vote-winning treatment. No surprise if she's
    So often, decades earlier, to be found
Head bowed, hands clasped, or silent on her knees

And inwardly to double business bound
    Since destined now (she knows) to be the one
Who'd teach them all those principles of sound

Soul-management that father had begun
  By laying down for the concentric spheres
Of chapel, home and shop. That's why she'd stun

The global commentariat in years
  To come by taking as her guiding light
A household politics where all frontiers

Like those set up, as if by natural right,
  By Keynesian economists to flag
The private/public line would soon invite

Her stock response: just take your shopping-bag,
  Compare the goods and prices, figure out
The best deals you can get, be sure to tag

All items carefully, and then you'd flout
  That whole perverse doxology that held
It vulgar simple-mindedness to tout

Such homely wisdom as a lesson spelled
  Straight from the shopping-list. Think too, since it's
A thought one's irresistibly impelled

To entertain, how perfectly this fits
  With everything she'd later do to show
The male establishment she'd grabbed all its

Macho prerogatives so there'd be no
  Conforming to the usual stereotypes
Of womanhood. Hence her resolve to go

That extra mile and silence all the gripes
    Of those who said she'd lack the element
Of grit or sheer cold-bloodedness to wipe

Her conscience clear each time her actions sent
    Some workforce home, some taskforce out to kill
And be killed, some directive to torment

The consciences of those who did her will
    And knew the human costs, or a quick nod
To the Joint Chiefs of Staff that they should spill

Enough blood to convince the awkward squad
    She saw things their way. Hard not to conclude
That something like her father's vengeful God

Of petty-bourgeois rancour made her brood
    Incessantly on old wrongs and project
The retribution onto those she viewed

Either as foreigners whom you'd expect
    To act like that or "enemies within,"
Like striking miners. These comprised a sect

More dangerous by half since their chief sin,
    In her book, was the kind that tore apart
The bonds of nationhood and laws of kin

By the fifth-columnist's satanic art
    Which, for her father's daughter, always loomed
Largest of all those lessons at the heart

Of Judaeo-Christian culture that foredoomed
    Some prophets, tribes or nations to be sold
Into captivity while others, groomed

For the lead roles in scripture, joined the fold
    Of God's own folk. It was her father's voice
That echoed in the history they told,

Those old blood-curdling tales, and in the choice,
    When ratings slipped, to take her chance on war
As a well-known restorative. "Rejoice!,"

Her victory-message said, which meant: ignore
    The near one thousand combatants who died
On both sides, and especially the more

Than one third of them drowned or fried
    In the old crate *Belgrano* even though
The best intelligence placed it outside

The danger-zone and sailing on a slow
    But steady course that took the ship far clear
Of anywhere its feeble guns might blow

A hole in her grand strategy to steer
    The nation back onto the course of true
Blue values that transcended all such mere

Facts of the matter. So, if we ask who
    Should, in the longer view, be held to blame,
Then working out which guilty foot the shoe

Fits least toe-pinchingly is not a game
  Best played by asking simply who did what
In legalistic terms that link up name

With deed as if through some tight-fastened knot
  Of straightforward agency. This fails to see
How few of the coordinates that plot

Our own life-histories are such that we
  Can trace them back to origin and just
How many of them, subject to i.d.

Checks of a stricter kind, are such as must
  Be put down to some shaping power that far
Exceeds the furthest bounds of what we'd trust

As hitched securely to the guiding star
  Of unique personhood. One standard way
Of taking this is lowering the bar

Of moral judgment so that we can say,
  In any given case, let's just allow
That *tout comprendre, c'est tout pardonner*

Since, everything considered, we can now
  Much better understand that it was well–
Nigh inescapable she'd turn out how

She did. This means, should we elect to dwell
  Intently on it, that his favourite line
Of pulpit-talk, his images of Hell

Mixed in with thoughts on how best to combine
    True godliness with making all you can
Along the way, must lead us to assign

Her to a cool bit of the frying-pan
    And not straight to the fire. Yet that's to stretch
Forgiveness to a point where it would span,

If need be, every human vice and fetch
    Up some fresh mitigating circumstance
With which attorneys might begin to sketch

A case for the defence. Then they'd advance
    The cause of all whom adverse fate had left
With few of life's advantages, or chance

Had thrown into a childhood world bereft,
    Like hers, of everything that might have saved
Them from that home-and-chapel-sanctioned theft

Of what, for others, all too briefly staved
    Off adulthood's arrival. We must track,
It's clear, some middling course between depraved

Since all-excusing attitudes that lack
    The blame-idea and others that accord
Zero allowance to the way things stack

Up early on and right across the board
    For those whose chief misfortune is to get
Themselves born into just that unexplored

Since deeply unappealing social set
　　Where piety assumes the sullen guise
Of lifelong forced sobriety and yet

Offers sufficient leeway to devise
　　Some handy tricks of conscience. These would leave
It free to pick and choose which rule applies

In cases where adopting a naïve
　　Or literal view of gospel truth could pose
Large problems, as when trying to deceive

One's business rivals, leading by the nose
　　Some unsuspecting customer with cash
To spare, or keeping colleagues on their toes

With memories of how matron used to thrash
　　Them back in public school (such were the joys!),
Or thinking it good policy to trash

That ship with its four hundred men and boys
　　Rather than let a UN peace-plan wreck
Her god-sent chance of war to quell the noise

Of those at home who'd get it in the neck,
　　Like those at sea, if only she could fix
Things there as easily as from the deck

Of a Class-10 destroyer. These were tricks
　　She'd picked up unawares yet by a keen
Observance, Maisie-like, of that which sticks

From childhood through the sundry shifts of scene
    In later life when lessons in their use
For ends of state will turn out to have been

(Since, so we're told, more intimate abuse
    Was kept for shop-girls) the most lasting mark
Our Grantham grocer managed to produce

Beyond the chapel-door. Soon she'd embark
    On the long quest for what might bring her power,
At last, to spread the message of his dark-

Side Manichaean gospel with its dour,
    Self-implicating knowledge of how sin
Must shadow every act and thought of our

God-haunted lives. If all great crimes begin,
    As some would say, in childhood's auguries
Of innocence undone, who'll think to pin

The blame down finally as hers or his?

NAUGHT FOR YOUR DESIRE

Viruses like Ebola are notoriously sloppy in replicating, meaning the virus entering one person may be genetically different from the virus entering the next. The current Ebola virus's hyper-evolution is unprecedented; there has been more human-to-human transmission in the past four months than most likely occurred in the last 500 to 1,000 years. Each new infection represents trillions of throws of the genetic dice.

—Michael T. Osterholm, *New York Times*,
September 11, 2014

Whichever way you look at it we're fucked.
   Even if a mutant virus doesn't kill
The lot of us this time because we've lucked
   Out yet again the next mutation will.
So if we get to feel like we're brands plucked
   Safe from the flames by a benign fire-drill,
Let's not use this occasion to construct
   Some providential creed meant to instil
A sense not merely of our having bucked
   The lethal trend (as we might do until
Our luck runs out) but of our being tucked
   Up tight by one who wards off every ill
The gene-pool throws at us. High time we shucked
   That childish mindset as the overspill

Of an old creed that ruled we all conduct
    Our lives as if by preternatural skill
At offsetting the human goods we'd chucked
    Back in God's bonfire as against the thrill
Of knowing he'd ensure we're never sucked
    Back in there with them, roasting on the grill

Of all things mortal. Where the bottom fell
    Out of that fine belief was when we hit
The crossing-point from letting ourselves tell
    A tale of times to come that could admit
At least some chance it might just turn out well
    To knowing tales like that were full of shit
Since nothing else could quite explain the smell
    Their telling now gave off. What best befit
Our brave new world are chronicles of hell
    Retold so as compactly to transmit
The message that we'd better promptly quell
    All thoughts that anything might come of it,
That wishful creed that managed to compel
    Our one-time selves and gave us hopes to pit
Against the harsher knowledge whose dark spell
    Now looms on every hand. So we'd best quit
The stale pretence that served God's clientele
    Reliably enough as holy writ
But now persuades us only to rebel,
    Like Shelley's Satan, *contra* the whole kit

And God-obsessed caboodle of a creed
    That has no room for all the things that may
At any moment, like some mutant breed
    Of pathogen that tweaks our DNA,

Go airborne finally and so succeed
    In knocking all the spirit-props away
For good and all. Where once it guaranteed
    Those hopeful types a fighting chance that they,
The happy few, might be found fit to plead
    Exemption come genetic Judgement-Day
Now they find that assurance of God's speed
    And health in soul and body fail to stay
Their joint collapse as errant genes misread
    A nucleotide and start the mortal clay
On its quick trip to nowhere. So they bleed,
    These Shylocks in reverse, as if to say:
We thought blind trust would cover every need
    And keep the viral horror-show at bay,
For us at least, but now it seems that we'd
    Too gladly let ourselves be led astray

By thinking our lot must be on the side
    Of some *Wirklichkeitsprinzip* more benign
Than any of the evidence supplied
    By those—medics, virologists, front-line
Observers all—whose working notes provide
    A darker estimate. If they incline
To take Ecclesiastes as their guide
    When asked by some reporter to assign
The odds, it's not so much the woe-betide
    Mentality that prompts this saturnine
Response but knowing how they're multiplied
    Each time around when segments recombine,
Swap bases, cross-encode and subdivide,
    So that the chance of things turning out fine

Is close to zero. Then the nucleotide
  Imperfectly transcoded shows cloud nine
To be the place we normally reside
  Until those mind-props, human or divine,
Give way to facts and figures that we'd tried
  To keep unfocused lest they intertwine,

Like mutant viruses, and interfere
  By their malignant chemistry with all
The self-protective ploys that let us steer
  To calmer regions. For the next close call
Might just be that which crosses the frontier
  Between what's close and what's apt to forestall
Our last defensive strategies since we're
  Now far too conscious, after the long haul
Of human *versus* virus, that "all clear"
  Means "got this latest bugger to play ball
For weeks, or maybe months, but best not cheer
  Too loudly since the due-dates tend to fall
More quickly as the viral forces gear
  Themselves up more intently for the brawl
With hi-tech medicine." So, whether near-
  At-hand enough for tidings to appal
Us daily or much farther off, the sheer
  Long-run dead cert still holds the mind in thrall.
"I have mislaid the torment and the fear"
  Wrote Empson, though the most devoted trawl

Through life and work won't much help to explain
  That cryptic line. My best bet: what he meant,
Or part of it, is how the lethal strain
  We know will one day fox or circumvent

The utmost of our efforts to contain
    Its wild proliferation wasn't sent
As any kind of torment, fear, or bane,
    Such as the shrewd Church Fathers might invent
(Here Empson once again) as "this last pain"
    In waiting for the damned. No god-squad bent
On retribution, just a complex chain
    Of DNA and RNA intent
To seize its opportunity and gain
    A foothold in the host-cell, having spent
Its time so far in the inert domain
    Of quasi-life where genotypes segment
Without remainder. If, then, we abstain
    From letting such reflections too much dent
Our sanity it's not because our brain
    Can't cope with notions that would else torment

Our every waking thought but more, as might
    Be Empson's point, because it's off-the-scale
Compared with other fears that tend to blight
    Our sense of human selfhood or assail
Our fragile self-composure. Best sit tight,
    The message says, and anyway not quail
At the mere thought of what may overwrite
    The very codes whose genotypic braille,
We once supposed, would stay in place despite
    Some one-off freak mutations and not fail
To keep the real mind-bogglers out of sight,
    Like how to keep rehearsing that old tale
Of human species-being and our fight
    Against the gene-invaders. For its frail

And faltering story-line's prone to invite
    Unwanted thoughts of how the genome trail
Leads back to where there's no such black-and-white
    Plot-structure and our mythoi won't avail
To screen out images that reunite
    Their chromosomes in nature's rummage-sale.

SCISSORHAND (MATISSE)

Drawing with scissors: to cut to the quick in colour reminds me of the direct cutting of sculptors

—Henri Matisse

Though produced by a very old man who was mortally ill, they seem to come from the springtime of the world.

—John Russell

It takes courage…to leave all props behind, to cast oneself, like Matisse, upon pure space.

—Fleur Adcock

The shapes came quick to hand, the colours too.
   They came like birds to Papageno's call.
A buffo role, but it would have to do.

The problem was, he had a job to haul
   Himself around and get a decent view
Of what he'd done. That's why he used the wall

To paste his cut-outs up, then took a cue
   From street-kids who seized every chance to scrawl
Their riotous graffiti where they knew

The stuff had greatest impact, shopping-mall
    Or boulevard preferred. His thought was: screw
The critic-gatekeepers who kept their hall

Of fame secure against that urchin crew,
    Plus high-art renegades like him who'd all
Make rainbows of the line those critics drew

Between the problem-works they'd soon install
    As 'late-style masterpieces' and the queue
Of reject candidates they deemed to fall

Beyond the utmost time-allowance due
    To culture-shock purveyors who might gall
Good taste but not for long. So if his blue

Nude cut-outs, four of them, can now enthral
    The art-world and entrance the critics through
A wonder-working power to do in small

And bright what drove *grands maîtres* to pursue
    Their deep and dark, let's once again recall
How the Salon de Paris and a slew

Of killjoy commentators cast a pall
    Across each mind's-eye-revelling shape and hue
He scissored out. Now that he's walking tall

In critical opinion and the few
    Dissenters mostly stow it or play ball
There's little thought of how these dazzlers grew

From a pent creativity in thrall,
    Like Ariel, to all things out-of-true
Since caught up in the death-defying brawl

Of mind with joint and muscle. So askew
    They were that now he'd lurch or cling or crawl
His way to show how paper-cut and glue

Might outdo all that age had done to maul
His body while he made the world anew.

AN EPISTLE TO MR. PHILIP GLASS

In that way Vinteuil's phrase, like some theme, say, in Tristan, *which represents to us also a certain acquisition of sentiment, has espoused our mortal state . . . . We shall perish, but we have for our hostages these divine captives who shall follow and share our fate. And death in their company is something less bitter, less inglorious, perhaps even less certain.*

> —Marcel Proust, *Swann's Way*, trans.
> Lydia Davis

This was the future, even if hardly anyone wanted to hear it. But, they were told, they shouldn't worry about that. Acceptance would not come right away, but the history of music was going down this road and you either got on the train or you didn't, . . . And if you didn't get on the train, you would be left behind.

> —Philip Glass

The consciousness of the mass of listeners is adequate to fetishized music. It listens according to formula, and indeed debasement itself would not be possible if resistance ensued, if the listeners still had the capacity to make demands beyond the limits of what was supplied . . . . The counterpart to the fetishism of music is the regression of listening.

> —Theodor Adorno, "On the Fetish
> Character in Music"

"What do you want of me?," asked Fontanelle
    In (so it seems) a passing fit of pique
When some sonata opted not to tell

The kind of tale that listeners vainly seek
    Once instruments take charge. This first induced
Mere puzzlement, then led to the mystique

Of memory's vagrant counterpoint that Proust
    Heard in his fictive *sonate de Vintueil*,
And now crows as its chicks come home to roost.

Let's ask: what might they want of us today,
    Those minimalist attractors of the rapt
Attention that piece only got by way

Of having so evocatively tapped
    A rich vein of *mémoire involontaire*
Rather than having qualities more apt

To gain it classic status. Just compare
    The Saint-Saëns or the Fauré works that might,
So scholars say, have done a hefty share

In sending Marcel off on his far flight
    Of recollection with (let's say) the sort
Of work that's now best suited to delight

Those types with a retention-time so short
    That anything beyond a four-bar riff
On rudimentary themes will quickly thwart

Their easy-listening grasp. For only if
    That theme turns up repeatedly on cue
And minimally varied will their tiff

With all things more demanding not undo
    Each *Leitmotif* and linkage put in place
By those composers willing to eschew

Such audience-appeal as comes by grace
    Of stretching ears and minds no further than
Allows distracted listeners to keep pace

With music matched to the attention-span
    Of ADHD toddlers. So let's pose
The question Vinteuil posed to Proust: what can

This music ask of us, or what disclose
    Of its designs on us as hearers fit
To listen, if the rule is: don't compose

The sorts of piece that might require a bit
    Of long-range structural listening or the kinds
That don't too soon or readily submit

To the ear's *Lustprinzip*. This bids our minds
    Resist the very thought that music should,
At times, break faith with any tryst that binds

Composers to ensure their works make good
    The aural non-aggression pact implied
By any music where it's understood,

On their as well as on the audience side,
    That here's no passage liable to tax
The listener's grasp. For else it flouts the tried

And tested maxim that whatever lacks
    Strong audience-appeal straight off is sure
To be the sort of piece that either smacks

Of an elitist culture once secure
    In its high citadel or stands revealed
As having nothing but the false allure

Of what's found to return the highest yield
    In culture-capital. So if there's one
Big question asked of listeners and concealed

Within the notes so effortlessly spun
    By minimalists (let's instance Philip Glass)
It's whether they're prepared to wish undone

The scheme of judgment that would have us class
    (Say) Haydn higher than the sundry heirs
Of old baroque, or think it merely crass

To give Spohr or Clementi equal shares
    With Beethoven of credit for what's come
Of music since that time. However there's

This question too: what if the vector sum
    Of those developments and all that tends
To offer moral optimists a crumb

Of comfort in bad times or buck the trends
   That breed despair is scrambled and reversed
By music that so pointedly depends

On listening-habits of the kind rehearsed
   In early childhood and thereafter trained
To want no more than jingles interspersed

With periods when, as somebody maintained
   Of Beckett's *Godot*, "nothing happens, twice."
The point's not that they must be addle-brained,

Those listeners, just that pieces which suffice
   To keep them musically content are such
As ask of them, by way of entrance-price,

That they should cultivate the common touch
   And kid themselves that what they're hearing rates
High on all counts. Then it may seem there's much

To say for epic length that modulates
   Predictably each hundred bars or so
And thus, by sheer inanity, negates

Whatever music might yet have to show
   Of such inventiveness as could transform
Its own expressive powers and let us know

Ourselves more fully. Granted, though the norm
   Of dissonance has lately been pushed back
To roughly where it was before the storm

Of progress blew from paradise to track
　　Its path from First to Second Viennese
Schools, this gives no good reason to attack

New-found simplicity as some disease
　　Brought on by failure of creative nerve
Or lazy-listener-led desire to please

With pre-digested formulas that serve
　　Its anaesthetic purpose. Yet it's not,
That dissident summation, such a swerve

From the joined-up coordinates that plot
　　How rapidly "new music" has switched course
From what once, at first hearing, took a lot

Of intellectual-auditory resource
　　From keen-eared types before they'd have a chance
Of grasping it to this full-scale divorce

Between the kinds of thing that might advance
　　Our sensory as well as mental powers
Of uptake and the kinds that so entrance

The hearer as to hold them rapt for hours
　　Through various well-tried forms of infantile
Regression. That's why these late-blooming flowers

Of post-Romantic decadence beguile
　　Them into something like the Wagner mode
Of semi-wakefulness, though in a style

Devoid of everything that Wagner owed
    To Beethoven and that ensured he kept
Harmonic tension high as tempos slowed.

This meant that those sufficiently adept
    At spotting leitmotifs and how they played
A structural-thematic role weren't swept

Resistlessly along and thereby made
    Complicit in the same kinds of on-stage
Stupidity and violence that betrayed

Wagnerian heroines to the insensate rage
    Of *echt*-Wagnerian heroes. Different when
It comes to minimalists who'd disengage

From an old dialectic that again
    Found voice in early modernism (think
Vienna, 1920s) since they'll then

Neither risk pushing listeners to the brink
    Of breakdown by emotions too intense
To bear, nor—worse still—seeing how they shrink

From structural complexities too dense
    To grasp while jogging, or when half-asleep,
Or shuffled on the iPod. Where suspense

Of chord or cadence once sufficed to keep
    Attentive audiences on the *qui vive*
By tensed anticipation of a leap

To some new key, such things now tend to leave
   Unmoved those whose diminished powers of long-
Range listening stretch so far as to perceive

Nothing beyond the time-span of a song
   On that same iPod even though the piece,
Like most of yours, may still be going strong

(Or just still going) when its batteries cease
   To operate. So if Proust's odd request
Of Vinteuil seems a novelist's caprice

Or curious thought-experiment to test
   What his *roman à fleuve* presumes to ask
Of dedicated readers, when addressed

To you the question's more: is it the task
   Of music to become so structure-free
And effortless that anyone can bask

Forever in the sun since shifts of key
   Bring no dark clouds. What it maybe desires
Of practised listeners is that they agree

To be as mindless as the piece requires
   If they're not suddenly to find they've been
Deprived of something better by suppliers

Of such down-market goods. If there's more spleen
   About this verse-epistle than perhaps
You'd normally expect to supervene

In musical debate, excuse my lapse
    Of manners but don't hasten to excuse
The insult to intelligence that wraps

An hour's worth of the stuff one might well choose
    As background music for a dinner-date
Around a minute's worth they just might use,

Those true past masters, when a shifting state
    Of harmony or mood requires they fill
That time with passagework, then modulate

And so—what far exceeds the gift or skill
    Of their note-spinning progeny—redeem
Its triteness by then having it fulfil

The promise of some half-remembered theme
    That, first time round, quite likely struck the ear
As nothing special but now comes to seem

The key to everything. Proust's souvenir
    Of fleeting *temps perdu et retrouvé,*
His tea-soaked *petite madeleine,* is here

Precisely to the point although it may
    Appear off-target since the gentle tweak
Of memory's heartstrings brought by the Vinteuil

Sonata had to do with its unique
    And (unlike the dunked almond-cake Marcel
So savoured) quasi-verbal gift to speak

Such secrets as Mnemosyne can tell
    Only in structured form. That's why the sound
Of some small phrase or fragment may compel

The vagrant memory to cast around
    For its pre-intimations in a zone
Of meanings more precise than any found

In recollected sounds or tastes alone.
    And so *mémoire involontaire* unfolds,
For Proust, in ways most intimately known

Through music and the colloquy it holds
    With lifetimes spent in quest of that which time
May yet pluck vibrant from the cramping moulds

Of time-fixated habit. So what I'm
    Here getting at is how those who content
Themselves with less—like giving up on rhyme

And meter through desire to circumvent
    Such formal impositions—will thereby
Be giving up on everything that went,

Back then, most forcefully to give the lie
    To any notion that the only fit
Way present-day composers can apply

Their special gifts or skill is to submit
    Each work to just that principle of least
Resistance that requires it be a hit

With those whose satisfaction's much decreased
    By every slight departure from the norms
Discreetly though effectively policed

On their behalf by all the varied forms
    Of vox-pop taste enforcement. What they class
Good music's aptest then to be what warms

The hearts of listeners predisposed to pass
    Such works as listener-friendly, and to fail
The more demanding kind. So, Philip Glass,

That's why I've taken Proustian leave to rail
    At how your music manages to turn
The Vinteuil question round and thus entail

That any answer to it's one we learn
    Not on account of venturing out beyond
Safe waters to where deeper currents churn

The tonal depths. More, it's some pool or pond
    With surface quite unruffled by such thoughts
As else might prompt the listener to respond

With further questions rather than retorts-
    In-kind of just the formulaic type
To which the well-trained minimalist resorts

As sub-melodic brainworms gently wipe
    Out all last memories of how music fared
In better times. If, then, I seem to gripe

Too much about what's trivial compared
    With other things—and if indeed it's true
That problems duplicate, not halve, when shared—

Still I'd suggest the question's aimed at you,
    My fellow-listener, next time you retreat
Into that lotus-land whose scents subdue

Your mind, make criticism take back seat,
    And switch off all awareness of how far
This music goes in striving to complete

Their obsolescence. Though my note may jar
    On such nirvana-seeking nerves and fall
Way short of getting them to say au revoir

To the seductive, thought-quiescent call
    Of minimalism still it might succeed
In helping those less thoroughly in thrall

To its hedonic spell and so impede,
    For a short while at least, the downward drift
Toward *musique d'ameublement*. The need

For that's as striking as the Doppler shift
    Produced when music-history's revoked,
As here, in ways that open wide the rift

Between a hard-line modernism yoked
    To the emancipation of all tones
In the chromatic scale and feelings stoked

Against it by the multiplying clones
    Of Glass or Arvo Pärt whose music harks,
Reactively, right back to the bare bones

Of old tonality. So it embarks
    On strategies to over-write the script
Co-written by the sundry heirs of Marx

And progress-minded modernists who'd tipped
    As winners just those works that best brought out
How tightly history's dialectic gripped

The kinds of music they'd most keenly tout
    For what it told of conflicts, whether waged
Directly in some recrudescent bout

Of the class-struggle or obliquely staged
    (As theorists prefer) in subtle ways
Requiring that the music be engaged

Only by those whose discourse best displays
    Such mediating skills. No doubt there's room
Here for a counterpart to the malaise

I've diagnosed, that is, for works that plume
    Themselves (along with the elective set
Of standard-bearing acolytes for whom

They're chiefly meant) on cancelling the debt
    Art owes to pleasure, or—to strike a note
Less hedonistic—making sure we get

The maximal incentive to demote
    What gratifies the ear. Yet pleasure came,
Back then, not just from music's power to float

The boat of listeners hoping for the same
    Old aural comforts, but how it could take
Us into regions far beyond the frame

Of ear-accustomed indolence and break
    Its hold by tonal innovations more
Effective since not so inclined to make

A rule of disavowing all rapport
    With any temperament that's still attuned
To vibes they programmatically deplore,

Those holdout modernists. Yet music pruned
    Of tonal affect as a point of strict
Decree is apt to find itself marooned,

Together with its phalanx of hand-picked
    Promoters, in a situation just
The opposite of works that neatly ticked,

In minimalist fashion, every box that must
    Be ticked by music seeking to regain
The ear of audiences left nonplussed

By music of the other, more arcane
    Or ear-repellent genre. Hence the flip-
Flop pseudo-dialectic where a strain

Of throwback populism trying hard to skip
    Three centuries of change now coexists
In mutual though uneasy partnership

With a left-over vanguard that enlists
    Its waning energies more in the cause
Of showing how intently it resists

The siren-call of popular applause
    Than showing how it might at length achieve
And (the most vital qualifying clause)

Achieve on merit a long-term reprieve
    From short-term memory. Still it's much worse,
So Proust would have us think, to find that we've

Been hearing skilled executants rehearse
    The sort of music that, when billed a top
New work commissioned from the public purse,

First asks of us that we consent to drop
    All pre-existent notions of what's worth
Our listening-time. Then it requires we stop

Our ears against the rising tide of mirth
    That greets—or ought to greet—the nth reprise
Of a duff theme that, owing to the dearth

Of musical invention, has to tease
    Its paltry substance out through umpteen bars
Where not much happens. This then guarantees

Consumer satisfaction since it mars
   No pleasure serviced by the aural balm
Dispensed to drivers traffic-jammed in cars

And punctually supplied with stuff to calm
   Their jaded nerves by doses of FM
Relaxative. That's how your pieces palm

Their hearers off with what impresses them,
   Since pre-convinced, as offering the last word
In those sublime simplicities that stem

From innocence regained, but might be heard
   More aptly—if again we bear in mind
The deep self-questioning Marcel incurred

At Vinteuil's fictive hands—as so designed
   That early converts to them quickly lose
All sense of just much got left behind

In music's self-eclipse. So *je t'accuse*,
   And you especially, since it's the scale
Of your works that convinces listeners whose

Respect's won by sheer playing-time that they'll
   Derive more benefit from works that run
To full symphonic stretch than those that fail

In that respect through tendency to shun
   Such elevated forms in (as one might
Quite reasonably think) the way best done

By self-styled minimalists. For if, despite
  Their scale, those works yield nothing to reward
The keen-eared listener soon put off by trite

Ideas or by some root-position chord
  Interminably held then it's a moot
Point, surely, whether being amply scored

And of a length proportioned to best suit
  Performance as the second half of some
Big concert should entail that they dilute

Yet further what's already now become,
  Even in those *echt*-minimalists who stick
With short forms, music such as lets us plumb

Its structure, like its feelings, in a tick
  And—if so minded—figure out the means
Of their production by a bit of quick

Text-book analysis. Should those routines
  Turn out to be the very sort that fits
This music it's because their method screens

The duplex question every work submits
  To every auditor who's then compelled
To ask not simply how the piece acquits

Itself by their lights but what truths it held,
  And might yet hold, for listeners breaking through
To grasp the more exacting message spelled

Out to those restless souls among them who,
  As Nietzsche said, experience the fate
Of music like an open wound. If you,

Our maxi-minimalist, could once relate,
  If fleetingly, to something like Marcel's
Self-questioning response it might deflate

That penchant for the kind of form that swells
  In length and scale inversely with the drive
To leave no forms in place beyond those cells

Of sub-thematic stuff that then contrive,
  By repetition, somehow to convey
A sense that they're organically alive

Like so much replicating DNA.
  However—as the simile concedes—
This notion just won't stick since there's no way

Genes could equate to that which far exceeds
  The grasp of any sequencer and stands
To our genetic blueprint as our needs

For music's consolation trump demands
  For acephalic pleasures of the sort
Your compositions yield. It's this that brands

Them works that too assiduously court
  The easy-listener's favour and confess,
Between the notes, their mission to abort

All trace of music's impulse to transgress
    Those comfort-zones. Where once it gave fresh nerve
To human striving, now it would repress

Whatever bucks its smooth regression-curve,
    Or any intimation of what you've
Kept constantly in check. So you deserve

At least the thanks of those who'd seek to prove,
    On current evidence, that we're the fools
If we suppose that music's power to move

Our minds as well as hearts by breaking rules
    Of custom or good form might be the spark
That lights a flame beyond the music-schools

Since kindled by those minds against the dark
    Of mindlessness. Then let us not conclude
Too quickly that the only valid mark

Of music's worth is some beatitude
    Attained exclusively by intellect's
Preparedness to have its bearings skewed

By inchoate emotion or effects
    Of the soft power exerted by what earns
Acceptance just so far as it respects

The status quo. Let's think the flame still burns
    And, on the strength of that, let's think there's yet
Some extant cause to hope that music turns

Aside from the compulsion to forget
    Its *promesse de bonheur* and so abjures
Your music's promise never to upset

The habit of compliance that secures
    Its listeners' readiness to fall in line
With every muzac-ready bar that lures

Them on beneath its stupefying sign.

A MORAL VACUUM

Khalid Sheikh Mohammed, the self-confessed mastermind of the 9/11 attacks, was brutally interrogated countless times by the CIA following his capture in 2003. But while the methods the CIA used to break down their prisoner were well-worn, the way in which they pieced him back together was not.

Mohammed—who in more innocent days took a degree in mechanical engineering at a US university—asked his captors a strange favour: would they let him design a vacuum cleaner? And the word from CIA headquarters in Langley, Virginia, was, yes.

Having extracted a confession and everything else it could by duress, the agency's priority now was to keep their star prisoner sane. Perhaps in calmer circumstances he might have further, less time-sensitive information to divulge. And who could say, he might even one day testify at a trial, at which he would need to appear a credible and uncoerced witness.

In other words, his handlers had to repair the psychological damage inflicted by the waterboarding and other "enhanced interrogation techniques" to which he was subjected immediately after being captured. Gradually, his self-esteem grew. Britelite had a debriefing room where Mohammed held what he liked to call "office hours," lecturing his captors about his childhood, his family and his path to jihad and al-Qa'ida. Tea and biscuits were served at these occasions.

—The Independent, *Friday, July 12, 2013*

It seems his treatment got a little rough.
    Do what you like with him, their orders said,
Since the worst you can do's not bad enough,
    But don't forget: more use alive than dead.

And so his minders did the usual stuff,
    Took their complete immunity as read,
Then made the most of this great chance to duff
    Him up now that they'd got the go-ahead.

The problem was, the guy turned out so tough
    And torture-proof that their lot just saw red,
Ignored all that don't-kill-the-bastard guff,
    And looked dead set on wasting him instead.

This meant the use of sundry off-the-cuff
    And ratcheted techniques that quickly led
The Pentagon to fear he'd sooner snuff
    It at their hands than have the rumour spread

That he'd cracked after all. Let them be taught
    A gentler way, ask him what might best heal
His psychic wounds if not the other sort,
    And, just to keep him on an even keel,

Enquire what kind of therapy he thought
    Would help him most effectively to deal
With having not so long ago been brought
    Close to death's door by their excessive zeal.

So that's the sweetener those guys offered: short
    Of freeing him or letting him appeal

Against these practices in open court,
    They'd try to fix things so that he might feel

His sanity restored rather than thwart
    Their purpose by declining to reveal
What more he knew, or else by the resort
    To babbling incoherence, whether real

Or feigned. When he came up with his request
    It's likely they surmised this was the case
Since, after giving it much thought, the best
    Way to get his head clear of that bad place

(He said) was to design and put to test
    A vacuum-cleaner from the database
Of those he'd studied years back with a zest
    For cleanliness that occupied the space

Now claimed by godliness. We glean the rest
    From what's let drop from time to time by grace
Of sources, CIA among them, blessed
    With warrant to dissimulate all trace

Of doings we'd be hard put to digest,
    As 'concerned citizens', if made to face
The facts head-on with no ruse to divest
    Them (and ourselves) of all that might disgrace

Freedom's fair name. In which case we'll perhaps
    Seek partial absolution in the small
Though welcome chance that this was just a lapse
    Of discipline, or else try to forestall

Our nagging conscience with the thought that chaps
    Like that have their own backs against the wall
In hotspots missing from the moral maps
    Drawn up for those, like us, who find it all

Too much and hope they'll keep it under wraps
    Rather than let such brutal truths appal
Our tender consciences. If something snaps
    In them from time to time, or what they call

"Enhanced interrogation technique" taps
    Into some vein that otherwise we'd call
Downright barbaric, then it's just those gaps
    In our quiet lives that keep us lot in thrall

(Or so we tell ourselves) to value-schemes
    Or moral codes that may be just the thing
For *bien-pensant* couch liberals whose dreams
    Of pure, uncomplicated justice cling

To past ideals and balk at any themes
    From a nightmarish present. Yet the sting
In such an attitude (although it seems
    At least a half-way decent ruse to bring

Relief from those soul-harrowing extremes)
    Is how it tempts our consciences to string
Along with what the water-boarding teams
    Took as their ready-made excuse to wring

Truth out of him as if the end redeems
    The chosen means by any trick to swing

The calculus in ways that brute regimes
    Have always found most conscience-quieting

Should doubts arise. Then comes the screwball bit
    That made the headlines: how his one desire—
When word came through that now they'd better quit
    The rough stuff lest their prisoner expire—

Was that his torturers provide the kit
    That Khalid Sheik Mohammed would require,
Should time and straitened circumstance permit,
    In order to design what any buyer

Of top-class vacuum-cleaners might think fit
    For purpose. So as further to inspire
His wished-for change of heart the guards would sit
    Around, serve tea and biscuits, and enquire

Respectfully what special features it
    Might have, or whether they could one day hire
The thing, or: cleaners are a piece of shit,
    So why not give the world a new spin-drier?

Still it's worth asking what might lie behind
    His choice if not (as most reporters found
It prudent to suppose) signs of a mind
    Either unhinged by guilt or losing ground

To distant memories of tasks assigned
    Way back when his grad student skills were crowned
With worldly recompense. This homely kind
    Of moral saw may strikingly resound

With vox pop and yet leave us apt to find
    Its leaky vessel running hard aground
On shallow sentiments we're disinclined
    To take on board whoever may propound

Them, whether pious editorials signed
    By lying hacks or journalists renowned
For having their high principles defined
    By loyalty to the biggest crook around.

So let's admit the issue's not just one
    Of blood-crazed lunatics, though this may suit
The purposes of *Daily Mail* or *Sun*
    Reporters as a handy substitute

For truthful headlines editors won't run
    When jobs are on the line or suchlike brute
Realities obtrude. One tale not spun
    By them concerns that episode en route

To 9/11 when he'd first begun
    The plan to cleanse all things that might pollute
His soul despite its fixed resolve to shun
    Each speck of dust like the forbidden fruit

That, soon as tasted, left that soul undone
    And mocked its one vocation: to refute
The infidel or show the world what's won
    Simply by staying true to the pursuit

Of spotless self-perfection. Then we might
    Find time and fresh incentive to re-think

Those vacuum-sealed ideas of wrong and right
　　That vetoed all our vain attempts to sync

Two such brain-stunners: how Domestic Flight
　　175 could vanish in a blink
Of pure apocalypse, and how delight
　　In cleaning dust and dirt from every chink

In US homes could finally incite
　　Such righteous zeal as pushed him to the brink
Of mayhem and beyond. Thus black and white
　　As moral colour-scheme looks prone to shrink

The options down too far and leave it quite
　　Beyond us to work out the Hoover link
(Appliance, not J. Edgar). That's the slight
　　Though vital tweak that might undo the kink

In our own moral wiring or the blight
　　Of planks concealing motes that lets us wink
At crimes near home yet turn the screws down tight
　　On those kept under till they're kept in clink.

THE LINE OF DUTY (SESTINAS)

Of the 11 undercover police officers publicly identified, nine had intimate sexual relations with activists. Most were long-term, meaningful relationships with women who believed they were in a loving partnership....Jenner, who had a wife, appears to have lived more or less permanently with Alison, rarely leaving their shared flat in London....It was an arrangement that caused personal problems for the Jenners. At one stage, he is known to have attended counselling to repair his relationship with his wife. Bizarrely, at about the same time, he was also consulting a second relationship counsellor with Alison.

—The Guardian, *March 1, 2013*

I sometimes wonder, but it doesn't do
To bring the topic up. In any case
He rings me every three days while he's gone
And lets me know each time he's coming back,
So I can tell the kids and count the days
And wonder where he went but never ask.

His wife and kids, I wonder if they ask.
I sometimes think about them, what they do
When he's away from home, how all the days
And nights go by while he's out on the case,
Although our team's devised all sorts of back-
Up stories for the whole time he's been gone.

This time it's seemed an age that he's been gone
But now he's here again so let's not ask
Him awkward questions. Nice to have him back,
Though my friends ask me: what does that guy do
In his months off? Suppose it's just a case
Of needing other stuff to fill his days.

He seems to be away much more these days,
Although I checked the dates and he's been gone
Less than a month this time. Still, just in case
He turns up suddenly, I thought I'd ask
The kids to maybe think what they could do,
The next time round, to welcome Daddy back.

Routine report: informant says he's back
With her, the suspect, hanging out most days
With that lot while they're planning what to do
For next week's anti-fracking march. We've gone
Out of our way so as not to have to ask
How she fits in. Still it's a dodgy case.

I've come to the conclusion he's a case
Of chronic itchy feet. This time he's back
And beating all about the bush to ask
If he can hang out for the next few days
With my lot. Better now than if he'd gone
When there was that "who snitched on us?" to-do.

No word for weeks now, and I find most days
I know it's just the case he's upped and gone,
Rather than ask "come back" as some might do.

★ ★ ★ ★ ★

Feel a bit shitty, but it doesn't do
To brood about it now that the whole case
Looks like collapsing. If the thing had gone
To plan and I'd brought all that info back,
Then cut loose just before the court-room days
No hack reporter would have thought to ask.

Funny, she seemed too politic to ask,
Or seemed to think the best thing she could do
To stifle doubt was occupy her days
With yet more eco-warrior stuff in case
Her nights brought all the missing details back
To frame the unasked question: where's he gone?

Or did she maybe figure where I'd gone
And why, but play along because to ask
The question squarely when I next came back
Would have kicked off the kind of how-d'you-do
That meant me being booted off the case
And you left one guy short on demo days.

Won't say I don't have rotten-feeling days,
Now that it's plain to see how things have gone
All pear-shaped with the prosecution case
As well as nearer home, or homes. Don't ask
Me stupid questions like "What will you do
To make amends?" because I'll bat them back.

And yet I have these dreams of going back
To her again, like on the magic days
When we two really clicked, and then I do
Some pretty stupid things. In one I've gone

Back to her (our) old bedroom and I ask:
Please take me back and then we'll drop the case.

Still, sentiment aside, if it's the case
That keeping my old job means going back
To under-cover work, they needn't ask
Me twice. Truth is, most of my time these days
Is spent just wondering where the passion's gone
And what those crazy friends of hers might do.

I watch him thinking, like he used to do,
Back then, about some case, but how it's gone
With this one I've not dared to ask for days.

AN INTERMITTENCE

Three years apart, and yet it might as well
    Have been three weeks, or days. Although the old
Adage applied, that only time would tell,
    This time in truth the only truth it told
Was of time's self-undoing. For we fell
    Back into thoughts and word-ways put on hold
Through all that time, and so conjured a spell
    That freed us, old lags suddenly paroled,

To take the tale up just where I'd cut short
    Its proper term. I grant you, some stuff went
On happening, we have it by report,
    And there's some evidence that we two spent
Those six years doing all the usual sort
    Of real-time filling things. Still no event
From that blank interim's the kind to thwart
    My time-sense like these signs of time's intent

To tweak our chronotope and so excise
    That merely clock-watch interval of *vie*
Quotidienne. This might perchance advise
    Some love-struck onlooker, like Donne's, that we
Could perfectly embody his surmise
    As touching that atemporal ecstasy
Of two that some few thirds may recognize
    By kindred gift although the rest agree

With common sense in apperceiving small
　　Change outwardly (here quoting Donne again)
To mark where time's hiatus might install
　　That lapse of years. The seven sleepers' den
Is where the poet fancied it should fall
　　With love's long slumber broken now and then
By waking dreams lest sleep too far enthrall
　　His soul and still the motions of his pen.

Long ways around I've gone so as not to dwell
　　Too closely on that border-zone patrolled
By time-lords every bit as keen to sell
　　Us back into time-slavery as scold
Time-wandering Proustians or threaten hell
　　For Platonists who'd force time to their mold.

Why, then, this temporizing last resort
　　To theory-talk when really all I meant
Was to convey how time-scales may distort
　　In life-redemptive ways? Yet that's the bent
That launched me on this replay of Freud's *fort/*
　　Da game, and speculation may have lent

The thing some real truth-content in the guise
　　Of thoughts more abstract only in degree
Than chunks of homely wisdom like "time flies,"
　　Though with this complication: that to see
The point, what you'd most need to analyse
　　Was how time lacked or lost a master-key.

Our vows said we were in for the long haul
  And if, though apostate, I say amen
To that it's not a prayer that should appall
  The faithful. Else no figuring how when,
Six years on, chance contrived this curtain-call
  It looped our time-line like Proust's madeleine.

EPITHALAMION: FOR JENNY AND DAVE
                                    (Santorini, July 2015)

Well, Jen, it's time things went from good to bad,
    Or (if you're dreading this) from bad to worse:
Time for your big-occasion-wrecking Dad
    To do his father-of-the-bride in verse.

How better celebrate the great event
    That brings your friends, your family and these
Well-wishers here to bless the time they've spent
    With you and Dave as happy invitees

To a match made in some place that's as near
    Heaven as makes no difference. And you look
So lyrical in all your wedding-gear
    (Not the best phrase, I know) that any book

Of great epithalamia wouldn't get
    Top marks unless it gave you pride of place,
The two of you, and by so doing let
    The world know how things ought to be in case

The world forgets.
              To Santorini we've
    Now come and it's a knockout, just the spot
For future hopes that aren't just make-believe
    But tried and proved already through a lot

Of shared life-history. Such a friendly bunch
        They are, these local people, though they've had
To put up with a full-scale credit-crunch
        And economic ruin through a bad

Conspiracy of nations they might well
        Have blamed on us. Then we'd seem just the kind
Of visitors who turn up for a spell
        In paradise or great chance to unwind,

Especially since exchange-rates make the whole
        Greek wedding-package currently a snip
For bargain-seekers happy in the role
        Of roving creditors who'd asset-strip

The glory that was Greece. Though that's as far
        As could be from our wedding-plan, it speaks
Well of these folk that nothing's come to mar
        The *entente cordiale* between Brits and Greeks

So that—whatever cynics say—one gets
        The feeling everyone's somehow a part
Of our rejoicing and the culture lets
        No shade of the economist's black art

Fall on our nuptials. Let's not press too hard
        On this but life's hard locally, and there's
A sense I have that Jen and Dave regard
        Their choosing this place as a choice that bears

As much on facing life with all the strength
        Their partnership affords as on the dream-

World recollections that will last the length
    Of all their years together. It's a theme

Quite suitable for verse, I thought, and then,
    Why let so perfect an occasion go
Unsung?, and anyway, good-hearted Jen
    Won't mind if I come on and spoil the show.

Of course it's famously a time to dig
    Around for family anecdotes that make
The speech sound like some chronic stand-up gig
    With brother-in-law stories (sorry Jake!)

And tales of—let me pluck one from the air,
    Just one of many—how on the Sealink
Ferry a bunch of stray kids asked us "Where
    Can we find Jenny *Power*?," which made us think

That maybe you were destined for great things.
    And so you were, and so I'm here to say
In due course, once this speech of mine takes wings,
    Though first more anecdotes to clear the way

For take-off.
            Jen, you always got my jokes
    Way back from early childhood, which struck me
As a great virtue, since I'm one who pokes
    Fun when he can and dearly likes to see

The point picked up at once, as on so many
    Occasions when some jest or other drew
A welcome sign it wasn't lost on Jenny,
    Or other times—I treasure them—when you

Perceived the comic side of things that we'd
    All failed to grasp. That's why no qualm deters
Me from a joke that surely must exceed
    The limits of good taste for connoisseurs

Of wedding conduct, namely one I'd planned
    To use when I was father-of-the-bride
To Clare, but which (I'm pained to say) was banned
    By everyone except—and this point I'd

Here like to emphasize—the very one,
    Our Jenny, who at that time thought it might
Go down quite well, but may now wish she'd done
    More to dissuade me. Granted, it's not quite

The sort of thing that custom would condone
    Even in these licentious times, but why
Let force of custom regulate our tone
    Through rules of good behaviour that apply,

If anywhere, then only where those rules
    Are drawn up to exclude the very thought
Of someone who, like Jenny, could make fools
    Of all the rulebook-sticklers.
                        Still I ought

To preface it with "Sorry, Jen" since she's
    Now looking slightly worried (who can blame
Her, honestly?) and thinking: no, Dad, please
    Not that one, or just hoping that I'll tame

The punchline, or recalling all those times
    It flopped, or someone didn't get the hang
Of it, or (as may happen with these rhymes)
    It came back at us like a boomerang.

So: it's about that time when Jen asked Dave
    If he'd give his opinion on the dress
She'd bought to go away in, and so save
    Her asking Clare or Mum to come and bless

Her choice of what to wear on honeymoon.
    Her question, "Do I look too big in this?,"
Addressed to Dave, came just a bit too soon
    For him to think, step back from the abyss,

And take the question straight. Thing is, she posed
    It coming from the bathroom framed against
An open door that instantly disclosed
    Her perfect figure, yet—although he sensed

The coming storm—he somehow couldn't check
    Himself before he said it: "Yes, but it's
Such a small bathroom."
                    Get it in the neck
    No doubt I shall, not Dave, which quite befits

The case since—let's be absolutely clear
    About it—poor old Dave in fact played no
Part in all this and it was my idea
    So crudely to debase the tone with so

Unsuitable a joke. I'll make amends
    Now, if I can, by trying to convey
What won't need spelling out for Jenny's friends,
    Who'll guess already what I'm going to say

Because they've made this lengthy trip to share
    Her great event and show not just how much
She means to them but how she's part of their
    Own past and present lives, and apt to touch

Those lives more deeply through her special gift
    For love and sympathy.
                I know you'll each
Have much to say of how she'd often lift
    Your spirits at some low point, how you'd reach

For Jen's phone-number when you'd been through some
    Life-crisis, or how far she'd go to try
And make things better. It's a gift I've come
    To recognize in her from years gone by

Right back to school-days when she'd always be
    Not merely "popular" but one of those
Who formed long-lasting friendships that would see
    Her mates through their recurrent highs and lows,

With Jenny just the one they'd always choose
    As confidante in both. I guess that's what
It took—putting yourself in others' shoes
    Like that—to let your colleagues know you'd not

Give up on your tough job, your work with all
    Those victims of man's inhumanity
To man, but make it something I should call
    A true vocation, if such vanity

Were not the sort of thing you'd think absurd
    And shut me up. At all events it's great
That you've spurned the big money and preferred
    To do the kind of job where you relate

To lives and people, rather than the kind
    That shuts them out.
                        Dear Jen, there's so much more
I'd like to say, but then you'd quickly find
    It just too much and silently implore

That I should now sit down. Just let me run
    On for a verse or two and say how glad
We are, your Mum and Dad, that it's begun,
    This marriage of true minds, this launching-pad

For our best hopes, since "Jen and Dave," along
    With "Clare and Jake," is now the sort of phrase
That sounds so right it cancels every wrong
    From way back. One thing missing in today's

Updated ritual was the bit that laid
    Down how the minister should ask the bride's
Dad—after telling everyone how they'd
    Best speak now of impediments besides

Blood-kinship of a Hapsburg type—if he's
    The one who's come to "give this woman away,"
Suggesting he's now lost the chance to seize
    Some inverse dowry that lot ought to pay

For his fair daughter's hand. It doesn't feel
    Like "giving you away" at any price,
Nor like some hard-negotiated deal,
    But more the kind of match that leaves us twice

Blessed with a son-in-law and daughter whose
    Devotion to each other simply shines
Out from them, though—like all the best-laid clues—
    It doesn't grab attention but combines

With everything about them so that now
    It's hard not to suppose they must have been
Predestined to meet up, or anyhow
    That some good angel must have overseen

Their life-lines all along.
               The thing that I
    Had most in mind (but went a bit off-course)
Was what a joy to raise our glasses high
    To Jen when she's so long been a huge source,

For Alison and me, of all the pride,
    The love and admiration that could go
To fill her parent's hearts. You want to hide
    Away out of embarrassment, I know,

When I say all this sentimental stuff,
   But it needs saying—if you'll just endure
One moment more—because you're apt to tough
   It out, or (more like) put the lid on your

Emotions and get on with what most needs
   Attending to at home or work. I think
That's a great thing about you—better deeds
   Than endless agonizing—but the chink

In all that psychic armor sometimes shows,
   And it's at just those moments you reveal
What's always seemed, to anyone who knows
   You well, how self-involvingly you feel

Their troubles in relation to your own
   Well-hidden yet no less demanding sorts
Of worry.
                    But enough: let's not postpone
The moment: contrary to all reports

My speech had a big point to get across,
   And it was just to say that Jenny's choice
Of Dave and his of her involves no loss
   For us but every reason to rejoice

With all our hearts. And so I bid you: pray
   Be now upstanding with me, raise a toast
To this loveliest of brides, and bless the day
   That, of all days, will always matter most.

THE BEAUTY OF IT

I would have preferred to have invented a machine that people could use and that would help farmers with their work—for example, a lawn-mower.

I didn't put it in the hands of bandits and terrorists, and it's not my fault that it has mushroomed uncontrollably across the globe. Can I be blamed that they consider it the most reliable weapon?

—Mikhail Kalashnikov

The beauty of it was how it would take
   Apart in twenty seconds flat, reveal
The bare mechanics, never jam or break,
   And so let first-time users get a feel
For how it worked. That's why my gun could make
   Of raw recruits sharp-shooters who can deal
With dicey situations apt to shake
   The nerve of those whose fancy guns conceal
All that mere nuts-and-bolts stuff for the sake
   Of slick appearances or sex-appeal.
They used to ask me: don't you lie awake
   In the small hours and see the blood congeal
On piles of corpses and not share the ache
   Of lost or shattered lives? But since the real
Blame lies with others, not myself, I'll stake
   My case on it: those wounds aren't mine to heal.

★ ★ ★ ★ ★

Not sleeping well just lately; it's my own
    Now close-up death makes what I've done acquire
Such haunting power. There's that discomfort-zone,
    That moral no-man's-land where those who fire
And kill bear no more guilt, if truth be known,
    Than those like me who aimed a good bit higher,
Strove for invention's accolade alone,
    And so bid conscience happily retire
As long as my invention helped postpone
    My day of reckoning. Now they all conspire,
Those untold deaths, so that at last I'm thrown
    Into such thoughts as question my entire
Life's work. When I unwrap this thing that's blown
    Whole dynasties away my one desire
Is to find some design-fault and atone
    For everything the death-squads so admire.

A DIFFERENCE OF VIEWS

Did Origen believe in the salvation of the devil? He clearly believed that all rational souls were able to be saved and this would, on Origen's view of the nature of demonic forces, have included the devil and his demons. So the accusation was stirred up that he taught the salvation of demons.

—*Robin Parry*

At that greatest of all spectacles, that last and eternal judgment, how shall I admire, how laugh, how rejoice, how exult, when I behold so many magistrates liquefying in fiercer flames than they ever kindled against the Christians; so many sage philosophers blushing in red-hot fires; so many tragedians more tuneful in the expression of their own sufferings; so many dancers tripping more nimbly from anguish then ever before from applause.

—*Tertullian*, De Spectaculis

God's mercy knew no bounds, or so it seemed
   To Origen, who put the case that Hell
Might still be empty since Christ's death redeemed
   All sins and sinners, even those who'd swell

Its ranks if all the candidates were streamed
   On stricter lines. His thought: since none can tell
What God decrees, why kid ourselves we've teamed
   Up with Him to select the personnel

For Satan's crew? Redemption-stories themed
    On mass-damnation warned him he should quell
That vengeful strain and be the one who dreamed
    That Satan could escape hell-fire as well

Since this might always be the message beamed
    By a wise deity whose blessing fell
Alike on those whom providence esteemed
    God's own and those predestinate to dwell

In darkness. Origen's idea looks all
    The nobler if you think how they preferred,
Those others like Tertullian, to forestall
    Such civilising thoughts in case they blurred

The line twixt saved and damned or Saul and Paul.
    'This I believe because it is absurd',
Tertullian said, and slammed the Christian ball
    Straight back into the court of those who'd heard

The sheep-and-goats stuff but been less in thrall
    To versions of it that more deeply stirred
The old blood-lust. So that we'd hear its call
    Ring loud and clear, Tertullian gave his word

That, if their heavenly joys began to pall,
    Then God's elect could watch the pains incurred
By those whose sins demanded they should fall
    Into the fiery pit that once deterred

The righteous who now fixed their downcast gaze
    On torments fresh devised and fit to cheer

Their jaded souls. To justify God's ways
　　To man or make His purposes appear

Less psychopathic might deserve high praise
　　From those, like Origen, of less severe
Doctrinal bent for whom *auto-da-fé*'s
　　On that scale don't too readily cohere

With what their own theodicy conveys
　　Of His benign intent. Yet why should mere
Compassion—now we hear Tertullian raise
　　His counter-claim—so dominate the sphere

Of judgment that its influence betrays
　　The same Old Adam who once lent an ear
To Eve's request and started the malaise
　　That came of letting human hope or fear

Dictate in matters where God's will alone
　　Should carry weight. So he, Tertullian, screwed
The stakes sky-high and set out to atone
　　For Adam's sin by sending Adam's brood,

Or most of them, to their appointed zone
　　In that vast torture-house where there accrued
All wages of all sins, all wild oats sown,
　　And every fall from grace God might include

In their last reckoning at the judgment-throne.
　　So, should some blessed soul be in the mood
For spicier stuff once Heaven's fare had grown
　　A trifle stale, their bliss was soon renewed

And heightened by reflecting how each moan
　　Sent up from Hell or glimpse of one who stewed
In seas of fire just might, if truth be known,
　　Be what brought final quittance for some feud

Long past. Since even blessed souls are prone
　　To gloat, those sounds and sights could be construed
As perfectly recapturing the tone
　　Of mother-in-law, or pleasurably viewed

As some old friend-turned-enemy now thrown
　　Below though rated tops by viewers glued
To his infernal pains. That this be shown
　　Quite fitting, though its fittingness elude

Less sapient types, was why Tertullian bent
　　His intellect to talking up that line
Of *grand guignol*. He wanted our assent
　　To pleasures that, should they lack such divine

Endorsement, we'd most likely represent
　　As plain sadistic or another sign
Of some perverse compulsion to invent
　　New tortures that exquisitely refine

The viewers' taste. Else they might soon relent
　　And think to question whether a benign
Or caring God could possibly have meant
　　His favoured few choice spirits to recline

At ease while, down below, their loved ones spent
　　Eternity where, by His sole design,

Each one at every moment underwent
    The very torments that might best combine

To conjure flat despair. Thus He'd prevent
    Their ever working up the moral spine
Not only, those who wished it, to repent
    But—those of Satan's party—to enshrine

"Non serviam" as flagging their intent
    To shove His edicts where the Sun don't shine
And pay no more instalments of rack-rent
    To God's slum landlords. Should the righteous pine

For something more appealing—less in hock
    To God's idea of how things ought to go
With miscreants—then building up the stock
    Of Origen might be one way to show

How stern Tertullian need not put a block
    On shared humanity, why letting go
Of Hell might leave no victims in the dock
    To face God's wrath, and lastly, apropos

Those tortures that enthralled the pious flock
    Of His elect, how switching such tableaux
For others less sadistic could unlock
    New springs of sympathy that might bestow

Such fellow-feeling as forbade them mock
    When told to by the Moloch-God. And so,
If you're out to apportion blame, don't knock
    Kind Origen who bucked the status quo

Of God-think in his time and caused such shock
  Amongst the orthodox that it left no
Choice for them but to reprimand, defrock,
  Or persecute those few who looked below

The radiant heights and saw what it denied,
  Their first Apartheid rule. It said: ignore
Those pleading voices from the other side
  Since why that gulf unless God fixed it for

His own good purpose: namely, to divide
  The chosen from the rejects, those who'd score
Sky-high on His account from those who tried
  But failed, or the massed legions of His *corps*

Glorieux from those whose agonies supplied,
  For some, the opportunity to pore
On torments of the flesh for souls enskied,
  Yet left some others yearning to restore

The human consanguinity that died
  When they renounced the flesh and so foreswore
All laws of kin. Take Origen as guide
  And then most likely you'll get over your

Desire that God's great plan should coincide
  With yours and have Him act as guarantor
Whenever someone else you can't abide
  Turns up for judgment and God wipes the floor

With their excuses since to see them fried,
  As per Tertullian, multiplies the store

Of heavenly joys. So Jekyll turns to Hyde
    And souls once trained devoutly to adore

God's mercy vow strict justice shall preside
    And sinners' pains be ratcheted the more
Excitingly the oftener they're eyed
    From heaven's vault. And yet, should we deplore

Such want of mere humanity or chide
    Their sub-angelic failure to abhor
That hellfire stuff, let's ask what bona fide
    Credentials we might have to claim *rapport*

With those who suffered, not with those who vied
    For front seats at the viewing. If "Encore!"
Strikes us as less than angel-like when cried
    After some episode of heretofore

Unequalled cruelty, should we not concede,
    Perhaps, on all the evidence to date,
That—looked from the nether side—this need
    To stress how fiercely we abominate

The stink of torture in Tertullian's creed
    And trust that Origen will put us straight
On Christian doctrine, might suggest that we'd
    Best think some more. Then we might see how hate

Takes many forms, how some of them may breed
    Compassion's likeness, and—to complicate
The reckoning further still—how this can lead
    To just such strange contortions as create

Those ecstasies of righteousness that feed
    Tertullian's fire. Should its heat once abate
Then finally we'd see that lack of heed
    To how these opposites could alternate

Insensibly was what near-guaranteed
    They'd end as two sides of a single trait
And so, once the machine got up to speed,
    Serve perfectly to show how church and state

Might profit by its workings and succeed
    At last in their long quest to sublimate
The whole shebang. Then nothing could impede
    Its course or hinder the conversion-rate

By which the gentle Origen, though he'd
    Allowed no vengeful cravings to dictate
His own theodicy, felt pity bleed
    Away and thoughts of mercy conjugate

With thoughts of how, should harsh Tertullian plead
    His case for mercy at God's bar, the gate
Of Heaven must close against him and God read
    The fatal sentence: change of heart too late!

Perhaps the sad truth is, no Origen
    To get us off that hook did not the shade
Of grim Tertullian hang above his pen
    And rule that he himself, God's scourge, be weighed

In a scale that would tip against him when
    Set up by his kind nemesis and made

To yield such unkind data as would then
    Ensure that any verdict thus displayed

Was one to which kind hearts would say amen.
    Always some bastard fails to make the grade,
Some cursed Malvolio slouches off again,
    And they get ready for the next crusade

By which to satisfy their burning yen
    For love while he reviles the masquerade
That shows why "cretin" stems from "chretien"
    And why Tertullian leads God's love-brigade.

NEOBULE AND ARCHILOCHUS:
AN EXCHANGE

Archilochus,...the earliest Greek writer of iambic, elegiac, and personal lyric poetry whose works have survived to any considerable extent. The surviving fragments show him to have been a metrical innovator of the highest ability.

Archilochus was famous in antiquity for his sharp satire and ferocious invective. It was said that Lycambes betrothed his daughter Neobule to the poet and later withdrew the plan. In a papyrus fragment...a man, apparently the poet himself, tells in alternately explicit and hinting language how he seduced the sister of Neobule after having crudely rejected Neobule herself. According to the ancient accounts, Lycambes and his daughters committed suicide, shamed by the poet's fierce mocking.

—Encyclopaedia Britannica

Neobule:

Archilochus, remember how your praise
   Of me not only spread the word of my
Rare beauty far abroad but helped to raise

Your lyric gift until it touched the sky
   And, Homer's equal, filled it with the blaze
Of god-like genius. Just recall how I,

Your dearest, quietly waited out the days
   Before our nuptials till, persuaded by
The urging of my father Lycambes,

At length I lost the courage to deny
   Your rival's suit. Why then these brute displays
Of savagery by which you daily try

To blacken our good family name, amaze
   The scandal-hungry populace, defy
All laws of common decency, and craze

Your ardent soul by stooping from its high–
   Bred martial strain to satire that betrays
A baser spirit. If, then, I decry

Your fickle muse that deems no caustic phrase
   Too harsh for me, nor stratagem too sly
For public use so long as it conveys

Your hatred and contempt, do not ask why
   This cry of pain since I'm the one one who pays
With my lost reputation while you vie,

You and those scandal-mongers, to erase
   All trace of it. Please know, as you let fly
With some new barb, that it may chance to graze

Your own good name since I'm resolved to die,
   Along with kith and kin, beneath that gaze
That now afflicts me with its evil eye,

Yet once—or so futurity portrays
   Your fabled gifts—could endlessly supply
New-minted lyric forms and diverse ways

To conjure what your love let you espy
   In me, like Galatea, through the haze
Of shapes awaiting life. Convert to lie

That long heart-cherished truth and nothing stays
   The same—no power of memory to tie
That time to this as your invective frays

Its few remaining threads and sends awry
   My every thought of you. But this delays
Three deaths that now must serve as our reply

Since nothing halts the genre-blight that strays
   From form to form till naught can satisfy
Your fiery soul unless it so dismays

Its victims that the strongest of them shy
   From public life as your communiqués
Insist: let honor go or bid good-bye

To life itself. If new-style satire plays
   The joker's role in all that hue and cry
Around our infamy then it obeys

Some god of hybrid forms that multiply
   Our sufferings as their chief device to raise
More laughter while the satyrs occupy

Old lyric's haunts and secretly liaise
    With our ancestral enemies to pry
Where its voice fails. Once we might euthanase

The hurt with lyric's salve, but should we try
    That now, reflected in the perfect glaze
Of your spite-polished art, then we'll supply

Some further jest that splendidly repays
    Your unrelenting wit. Spare me that sigh
You'll one day breathe as memory decays

Along with all the joys afforded by
    This crowning triumph of your comic phase
While still the momentary thought of my

Once lyric-feted loveliness essays
    Your satire-hardened heart. Yet know that I
And my poor kin no longer shall dispraise

Your name nor call down vengeance from the sky
    For our dishonor though you set ablaze
The pyre of calumny on which we die.

Archilochus:

It wasn't you, Neobule, but your
    Kid-sister I was screwing, so just quit

This endless litany of woe. What's more,
    Your father all along connived at it,
Said you were old enough to know the score
    And wouldn't take much urging to remit
Your nuptial rights. But, girl, should you ignore
    The call of duty and give us some shit
About lost reputation or implore
    The gods to punish me as you see fit
Then just be clear, I'll wipe the fucking floor
    With you lot so you'll never know what hit
Your dwindling clan. Tell Dad and tell that whore,
    Your sister, they're just nincompoops who bit
Off more than they could chew that day they swore
    They'd drag me through the dirt and dare to pit
Their tale against mine in this phony war
    For hearts and minds. The trouble with close-knit
Families and sibling bonds is how they store
    Up grievances that may start out legit
(Like yours, let's face it) but become a bore
    When it's required that everyone submit
To having the complainants daily pour
    Their sorrows out till listeners either split
Or split their sides. That old *esprit de corps*
    May once have been a handy piece of kit
When family names were still worth fighting for,
    But what's the point when a mere touch of wit
Can puncture noble pedigrees galore
    And one lewd epigram from some new skit
Of mine on wings of satire can outsoar
    The highest dignities? A moonlight flit
Will save my skin if your lot should deplore,
    And prosecute my stuff, but if you slit

Your throat right now then all their talk of law
    Won't heal the wound.
                Let me write your obit:

"Here lies Neobule, a maid who wore
    Pretend-virginity like a fake tit,
Whose sister banged me like a shit-house door,
    And whose insatiable, man-eating clit
Now rots with her false heart."

              Yet our *rapport*,
    Neobule, is still what spurs my wit,
Not just my taste for mockery and hard-core
    Pornography or readiness to sit
In judgment upon those with wounds still raw
    From my unsparing jibes. It's sacred writ
To me, this satire stuff, and helps restore
    The strange amalgam that all those lit-crit-
Trained genre-analysts may now abhor
    Yet one day will find reason to admit
As having helped Archilochus explore
    Such wild extremes that his satiric grit
And lyric pearls were of a piece before
    Good taste decreed their parting. *Floruit*
Archilochus, they'll say, when poets saw
    No ethical or formal deficit
In verse that just declined flat-out to draw
    Such tasteful boundaries or retrofit
The veering passions born of love's furor
    To genres born of love's surcease. *Dixit*
Archilochus: if you'd locate the flaw
    In lives and loves then see how it's backlit

By every lyric vision that forbore
To steel itself for satire's incipit.

BUDGET DAY, JULY 8TH, 2015

*Bankers want to see an easing of regulation after an increase
in red tape following the financial crisis. Osborne is aiming to
sound a conciliatory tone....According to the Financial Times,
allies of Osborne have said that the chancellor believes some
tax and regulation may have been excessive, but that it was a
politically necessary measure. Now with the election won and a
majority obtained, there is more freedom for change.*

—City A.M., *July 13, 2015*

Elsewhere the lingering life-hopes fade and die.
    It's all there in your red attaché-case.
But now's your glory-day, so hold it high.

Just please the fat cats and the CBI
    And you'll have no more conscience-calls to face.
Elsewhere the lingering life-hopes fade and die.

That lot, who once just managed to get by
    Won't now, but that's their own, not your disgrace
For now's your glory-day, so hold it high.

Just get the *Mail* to stop them asking why
    They always lose, or if you've fixed the race.
Elsewhere the lingering life-hopes fade and die.

What dies in them is all that goes awry
    When they're routinely caught out at first base.
But now's your glory-day so hold it high.

Just get the *Sun* to say they're all work-shy
    And then get all the loan-sharks on their case.
Elsewhere the lingering life-hopes fade and die.

If that lot cut up rough, you can rely
    On Channel Four to keep them in their place
After your glory-day, so hold it high.

And if some others say you're a bad guy,
    Trust Murdoch to ensure they get no space.
Elsewhere the lingering life-hopes fade and die.

So long as there's no lie-machine to vie
    With his, your lies are those that set the pace,
And now's your glory-day so hold it high.

Wave that attaché-case lest any try
    To question plans your banker-friends embrace.
Elsewhere the lingering life-hopes fade and die.

Should there be some life-hopers who decry
    Those policies, just sink them without trace
For now's your glory-day, so hold it high.

Maybe a few on your own side will shy
    From deeper cuts, but still you hold the ace.
Elsewhere the lingering life-hopes fade and die.

If they protest, then do it on the sly:
    You're Oxford-bred, just soft-soap them by grace
Of this your glory-day, and hold it high.

No matter if you don't see eye-to-eye
    With some old-Labour wielder of the mace:
Elsewhere the lingering life-hopes fade and die.

Truth is, your current budget's just a dry-
    Run raid on nine-tenths of the populace
For this your glory-day, so hold it high.

Neat trick, the one that lets you re-apply
    "Austerity" to have the term erase
Those lingering life-hopes that now fade and die.

Just tell the plebs they're welcome to defy
    Your new poor-laws but they're the ones you'll chase
On this your glory-day, so hold it high.
    Elsewhere the lingering life-hopes fade and die.

STRICT-FORM SESTINA FOR THE MARQUIS DE SADE

In this dream—even at the age of thirty-eight—Sade yearned for the embrace of a mother. "Oh my Mother!" he cried out to [Petrarch's] Laure, prostrate at her feet, as if he were one of the tortured victims of his own fictional erotic fantasies. But when, in his dream, he reached to grasp her, she disappeared and abandoned him to his lonely suffering.

—*Neil Schaeffer,* The Marquis de Sade: A Life

He knew (or should have known) they'd get him wrong,
   The moralists and those who took it straight,
His endless improvising on the one
   Big thing that mattered. Not that he was just
Inventing stuff for kicks, or getting off
   On kinky fantasies where thought of pain

Endured was bliss enjoyed. Let's face it, pain
   Was that big thing and so they weren't flat wrong,
Those literal-minded types, or too far off
   The moral point, those sticklers for the straight-
Forward message. Still what made them less than just
   In so concluding was neglect of one

Odd fact that should give pause—at least if one
    Doesn't page-hop to the next scene of pain
Inflicted or procured—for then it's just
    Conceivable that all our thinking's wrong
On this touchiest of topics. Read him straight
    By all means but recall those noises-off

He suffered daily—since a short way off
    From his barred gaol-cell window—one-by-one,
As Madame Guillotine dropped clean and straight
    To outstretched necks. Strict justice said the pain
Was wholly warranted as they'd done wrong
    And it, though *fort*, was scarcely *dure*, so just

And fitting. If our libertine thought just
    The opposite then we can best start off
By figuring maybe common sense is wrong
    To hold that, for the sadist, it's all one
Whether we're talking real or fictive pain,
    Whether those living torments taken straight

From Robespierre's book or those that issue straight
    From some odd neural kink that finds them just
To its inventive taste. So human pain,
    Where real or witnessed, turns the Marquis off
Through that empathic gift that makes him one
    With fictive beings whose imagined wrong

Goes straight to that raw nerve. What sets it off
    Then looks like just his crying need for one
More suffering soul whose wrong might cause him pain.

WIFE TO MR. HAYDN

The daughter of Johann Peter Keller that Haydn really married was Maria Anna Theresia Keller, who was born the seventh child of her parents on 25 September 1730....Since Anna Keller signed her marriage contract and her first will "Maria Anna" (names that were also part of Aloisia's name) and appears as "Anna" in other documents, the mistaken identity never became apparent in documents from Haydn's later life.

—*Michael Lorenz, "Haydn's Real Wife"*

Suppose someone said, pointing to Nixon, "That's the guy who might have lost." Someone else says "Oh no, if you describe him as the winner, then it's not true that he might have lost." Now which one is being the philosopher here, the unintuitive man? It seems to me obviously to be the second. The second man has a philosophical theory. The first man would say, and with great conviction, "Well, of course, the winner of the election might have been someone else..." So, such terms as "the winner" or "the loser" don't designate the same objects in all possible worlds. On the other hand, the term "Nixon" is just the name of this man.

—*Saul Kripke,* Naming and Necessity

So, room for hope: maybe she wasn't such
   A battle-axe, or apt to block her ears
And stomp off when the others came around,

Vanhal and Dittersdorf, and then (a touch
    Déclassé but top-rated by his peers)
That Mozart boy, the only one she found

Half-way agreeable or up to much
    Once they'd stopped playing, sunk a dozen beers
Between them, and agreed to let the sound

Of Josef's music (or the double-dutch
    They talked about it) silence any fears
That maybe this new *Wunderkind* was bound

To steal his show. Now it turned out that they'd
    Defamed her monstrously, the scholars who
Just went on trotting out that same old tale

About the constant misery she made
    Of Papa's life, but so contrived to screw
Things up it took two centuries to nail

The libel. Seems that all the old brigade
    Of musicologists believed it true,
The henpeck stuff, which led them without fail

To hand it down and so promote the trade
    In any rumour-mongering that might do
To place Frau Haydn on the Beaufort Scale

Of stormy wives. Truth is, the thing went back
    To his biographer, one C.F. Pohl,
Who (we now learn) took insufficient care

With note-keeping or else displayed a lack
    Of proper training in his chosen role
And who must therefore take the largest share

Of blame for a false trail which gave the pack
    Their scent of female prey. What blew the whole
Shebang sky-high was study (all too rare,

It seems) of certain records that kept track
    Of dates and details and so proved the sole
Remaining proof of how it failed to square,

That legend, with the chronicle of those
    Plain life-events set down with not the least
Small hint of myth or narrative intent

As births, deaths, marriages—whatever goes
    Toward the stock of knowledge that's increased
By every instance of the scholar's bent

For patient archive-grubbing where he knows
    Home-truths reside. So at this point they ceased,
The Haydn-seekers, to misrepresent

One candidate for wife and rather chose—
    Since new research had diligently pieced
The evidence together—to prevent

Worse damage from befalling the fair name
    Of *Haydnstudien* by making known
That, of the Keller girls, the one he'd wed

Was not Aloysia who'd achieved ill fame
    As his domestic scourge because she'd grown
To a mere eighteen months, the record said,

When some obscure mishap or illness came
    To cut life short. So Pohl & Co. were thrown
Off the right track by taking it as read,

That marriage-record, or supposing some
    Plain fact-transcriber must back then have seen
The entry, made a note of it, and checked,

If only by calendric rule of thumb,
    That the event might plausibly have been
As commonly set down. So the correct

Account—as scholars (most of them) have come
    Around to thinking—says that we demean
The cause of scholarship and disrespect

The name of that dead child if we're so dumb
    As not to grasp the truth: that our routine
Ideas about which hen it was that pecked

The kindest and most genial of all
    Our great composers have been way off-beam
Since almost the year dot. In truth his bride

Was that child's sibling whom they chose to call
    "Maria Anna" likewise, on a scheme
Straightforwardly if confusingly applied,

But then—as if half-minded to forestall
    Such errors once the error-spawning meme
Was up to its old tricks—put that aside

And settled on "Theresia" as a small
    Concession to the need that something seem
To make them different women or to guide

The suitors or the scholars in their quest
    For the right girl. So, you may say, what's here
Achieved is just a small but in its way

Impressive instance of how thought can test
    For such false reasonings as no doubt we're
Innately prone to and ensure that they,

If not eliminated or suppressed,
    Are then at least not given the all-clear
To work their mischief wholesale. Yet this may

Be deemed one sign of how they all invest,
    Those types, in the self-comforting idea
That some such well-judged putting-into-play

Of new-found evidence and clearer thought
    Might somehow wipe the record clean or shift
The burden of those long-accustomed jibes

About Aloisia's nearly having brought
    An end to his good-humour or so miffed
His well-tuned temperament that certain vibes

Might strike responsive ears as somehow fraught
   With echoes of the ever-widening rift
Twixt man and wife. For so it was the scribes

Of mainstream musicology once taught
   Their reader-listeners first to give short shrift
To Aloisia, then—to mark the tribe's

Belated turn to more enlightened ways
   Of thought—advised us readers we should take
An altogether different view and ditch,

Along with faulty scholarship, the craze
   For serving up the usual range of fake
Bit-parts and sexist stereotypes by which

That old-school musicology betrays
   Its male agenda. That's why, for the sake
Of some cheap joke, it casts her as a bitch

Whose legendary ill-humour then displays
   By contrast every gift that went to make
Her Josef, in his music, such a rich

Resource for anyone who'd ride them out,
   Those patches of domestic *Sturm und Drang*
Or suchlike contretemps. These might,

To lesser mortals, spell the final rout
   Of all that once united yin and yang
But, in his case, contrived to lift the blight

Of ages—or relieve the short-lived bout
  Of gloom brought on (let's say) by some harangue—
Through such a sense of darkness turned to light

As comes to solace grief and silence doubt,
  At least for now. Yet if the chorus sang
About these things in bars they always cite,

The commentators, from the opening strains
  Of his *Creation*, then the same applies
Elsewhere in ways less plain to hear yet still,

For many, what so perfectly sustains
  The truth of those domestic lows and highs
That he transformed, Prospero-like, until

Their formal interplay alone remains
  And keen-eared listeners can at best surmise,
By dint of fine-tuned analytic skill,

What subtly interwoven joys and pains
  May here find voice. So if they now revise
The old back-story so as to fulfil

Their scholarly vocation, it's no more
  Of a corrective to the way they'd spun
The tale of Haydn's genius than to read

The names "Anna Maria" where before
  They'd read "Anna Aloisia," while the one
Picked out as Josef's bride is now decreed,

By general assent, to leave the score
    Unchanged since still the source of old-style fun
With all the attributes that guaranteed

Her, like her sibling, as an endless store
    Of anecdotal chat. So what they'd done,
Philosophers might say, was just proceed

To switch the proper names but not enquire
    Too closely into how or by what kind
Of evidential warrant they'd accrued

Such power. Though new disclosures might conspire
    To shift the referent they still inclined,
The genial Haydn's less than genial brood

Of partisans, to stick with all their prior
    Convictions when, as usual, they'd a mind
Not to let awkward truths-of-fact preclude

Whatever fictive tale they might desire
    To put around no matter who's consigned,
Like her, to bit-parts of the sort eschewed

By self-respecting extras. Listen well
    To how his wit and humour always stage
Their peace-restoring comeback even though

He's maybe (who knows?) just been given hell
    Or else—a handy reference-point to gauge
Their differences—encountered moods as low

As any that, in Mozart, mean a spell
   Of dark G minor. These a later age
Would take as ample reason to bestow

On him, not Haydn, prior claim to tell
   Such inner-worldly truths as might assuage
Our music-wakened need to undergo

Those same upheavals of the human soul
   That (we suppose) must certainly have played
Their part in drawing out a music prone

To overwhelm our fragile flood-control
   Or bid Dionysus' retinue invade
Apollo's realm had he not also known

How most effectively to button-hole
   The form-attentive listener. What's conveyed
By Haydn's gently civilizing tone

Is more: steer clear of the magnetic pole
   Marked "tragedy" or "inner torment', trade
Your fraught dispatches from the danger-zone

For feelings nearer home, and wonder if
   Perhaps humanity, like music, stands
To gain far more by nurturing a sense

Of irony than letting some small tiff
   Gain resonance. The discord then expands
As dark-side harmonies grow more intense,

Or rows turn into struggles on a cliff-
   Edge looking out across the ruined lands
Where dazed combatants witness the expense

Of spirit as each rumour brings a whiff
   Of grapeshot. Like a laying-on of hands,
That trick of Haydn's somehow to condense

Fresh hope in every minor-major riff
   Or bring forth, from those ear-bewildering strands
Of sound, creation's aural hieroglyph.

WAVELENGTHS

Slowness and constancy; receptive openness to the environment; a passive, somewhat withdrawn character; a gesture of pulling in or retracting rather than projecting outward; being formed from the outside – each of these phrases emphasizes a slightly different side of a unitary way of being. We can, with inner effort, bring all the sloth's traits into a coherent picture that 'holds together'. And when we do this, we find that 'every detail can begin to speak "sloth"'. That is, we can recognize a 'slothness' that shines through all the details and makes them into a single whole.

—Stephen L. Talbott

While film buffs know Hedy Lamarr . . . for her roles in many classic films, she was also an accomplished inventor. Lamarr is best known . . . for a 'Secret Communication System'. The subject of the patent is a frequency-hopping spread-spectrum technology intended for a difficult-to-jam radio-frequency guidance system for torpedoes . . . . By transmitting on multiple radio frequencies, and switching frequencies rapidly (multiple times per second), the radio signals would sound like random noise to anyone monitoring any of the frequencies. But, with the sender and the receiver of the signal hopping frequencies simultaneously, the signal would be clear.

—Matthew M. Yospin

From his far vantage-point the pendent sloth
Looks down. The watcher's metabolic rate
Begins to quicken as she sees it. Both

Now undergo a certain change of state
Although the one is naturally loth
To let the woman's distant gaze dictate
Some correspondent quickening, while her growth
Of interest bids her freeze-frame and await

The sloth's next move. Truth is, I didn't know
What moral it should point, that little tale
Like some Aesopian fable meant to show
(At a first shot) how artefacts of scale,
Time-scale in this case, offer such tableaux
Of mortal finitude. It's what we fail
To grasp if we suppose that things must go
Along in concert or one beat prevail

For all despite those detours that accrue,
Those time-lapse intervals that came between
Their two attempts to have eye-contact do
World-bridging work. Then looks exchanged could mean
Things understood, instead of sent askew
Across the species-gulf installed to screen
Out any chance some message might get through,
Some signal flash up clear and so convene

The kind of freak assemblage that defied
Genetic codes or laws of natural kind,
As well as chronometric scales supplied
To keep genetic profiles well defined
And crosstalk filtered strictly on the side
Of background noise.

                Still, if she had a mind
To get on terms with him (the sloth, but I'd
An interest here) then likely she inclined

Toward the sort of wavelength-hopping ruse
Thought up six decades back by 'well-known star
Of stage and screen' - yet, it appears, one whose
Gifts far surpassed all that - Hedy Lamarr,
None other. She worked out how you could use
Such one-off channel-binding to debar
The enemy from tracking subs that cruise
The depths and scan the airwaves. Safer far,

These nonce liaisons, on account of their
Occurrence not requiring any code
That might be cracked but simply that they share,
Each time, the *Treffpunkt* of this episode
Where two devices conjugate and where,
Next thing, the system's ready to reload
And pick some other frequency to pair
Them off again. What this device bestowed

In time of war, as now, was just the trick
For keeping channels open, making sure
Stuff went from A to B, allowing quick-
Change backup codes, and plenty of secure
Alternatives lest something fail to click
Straight off.
                Suppose she manages to lure
The creature's eye while his slow seconds tick
Serenely by and her sloth-overture,

Its tempo set to last as long as she
Has staying-power to hold his steady gaze,
Endures for him just long enough to see
A gesture so ephemeral it stays
One moment on the vague periphery
Of consciousness, then fades to join the day's
Long list of things too transient to be
Recorded as sufficiently in phase

With his chronometry to warrant more
Extended notice. Room here for a spot
Of channel-hopping, maybe, since the score
Of sloth-to-human contact-hours is not,
So far, such as to promise a rapport,
A mutual kinship or a shared soft spot
Between them, but much rather to implore
Our pity for the optimistic lot

Who think – perhaps because, once in a while,
They've frolicked with the dolphins – that we're hard-
Wired to converse in rapt though wordless style
With any creature whom we catch off-guard
Enough and not inclined to run a mile
At our approach.
                        Yet maybe one trump card
Remained to our sloth-whispering cryptophile,
One that put them in touch because it barred

All access save to those who channel-hop,
Sit light to protocols, switch codes at will,
Prefer whenever possible to drop
In unannounced, and make a social skill

Of Hedy's ruse for doing whistle-stop
Traversals of the spectrum up until
The moment when two parties get to swap
Call-signs and messages, then start the drill

For channel-switch again. This means the next
Exchange eventuates as if through sheer
Contingency and linkers-up aren't hexed
By droppers-in who seek to overhear
What's going on, or suddenly perplexed
When some fixed channel oddly fails to clear
And messages bounce back. Yet what so vexed
The guardians of order through their fear

Of such illicit cross-talk was what gave
Hedy her notion: why not dump the whole
Fixed-wavelength thing, make channel-choice a slave
To random channel-drift, grant chance its role,
And – since the one thing all code-breakers crave
Is a fixed range of options to patrol –
Devise a system programmed to behave
As if the rout of systems were its sole

Objective, or its aim to substitute
For protocols an idiom that would ring
True just the once.
                              This set-up might not suit
The regimented types, like those who cling
To text-book rules whenever they compute
A wavelength, or sloth-fanciers when they bring
To each encounter senses less acute
For having drunk too deeply at the spring

Of sloth ethology and so confine
Their bandwidths to the narrow range that's set
By fixed ideas. These bid us draw a line
Between engaging in a tête-à-tête
With creatures, like the sloth, that we incline
To honor, even humor, since they let
Us fancy they'll wake up and take a shine
To us their watchers, and the riskier bet

On long-range outcomes that requires we place
Less trust in known technologies or modes
Of messaging. Then we may find the space
For human-sloth communing soon explodes
With possibilities once we embrace
The thought that every system over-codes
For errors of the sort that, could we face
Them squarely, might yet prove the very roads

That got us round some awkward traffic-jam
Or whizzed our under-coded message past
The filter.
                    Think of an old radio ham
Who's not got through to someone on his last
Few tries so now knob-twiddles (scan not scam)
And rediscovers something of that vast
Sensorium beyond the codes that cram
Our signals, whether radio mast-to-mast

Or sloth to human being, into band-
Widths so dense-packed that they can leave no room
For what may come of linkages unplanned
By any apparatchik set to groom

The airwaves. Yet we've had the means to hand,
Since Hedy's big idea, for putting whom-
Soever wishes in a spectrum-scanned
Though one-to-one rapport that lets them zoom

Unerringly to that one channel whose
Slot-occupier (on a strict pro tem
Arrangement) gets to hear the latest news
Or else communicates some perfect gem
Of intimate exchange.
                        This means the screws
Of waveband rationing are off for them,
Those open-access messengers who choose
Her therapy for all the ills that stem

From species-bonds or channels preassigned
As if by some necessity beyond
The grasp of channel-hopping types. They find
It irksome that the only sort of bond
That counts for much is one with power to bind
In forced relation, rather than respond
In ways that might obey a law of kind
More likely to accommodate the fond

Hopes vested in a chance, however small,
That Hedy's winning formula might hold
Across the board. Then there'd be room for all
Our criss-cross signal pathways to unfold
A full-range two-way spectrum where no call
Need go unanswered, nobody be told
Their call-sign's unacknowledged, and no trawl
Through bristling airwaves tell us we're controlled

By interests not our own. Else we might link
In common cause with those who, for the sake
Of shared humanity, refuse to think
Along the lines that our controllers take
To show our thoughts dependably in sync
With theirs.
                        If, then, the common cause we make
Is one that bids its devotees not blink
At these large claims, it's just because the stake

We have in it goes wide as well as deep,
Extending from a *dialogue des sourdes*
(Or so I thought since you two seemed to keep,
Woman and sloth, the slightest of accords
Between you) to a discourse that could sweep
Aside the barriers commonsense affords
So as to hold us back from such a leap
And maybe point us gradually towards

The moral shift envisaged, then repressed
With every step-change in the techno-sphere
Since Gutenberg and Caxton.
                        There's a test
Of this, you know, in all the ways that we're
Now finding to get over having messed
Things up so often, ways that interfere
With any 'natural course of things' but wrest
Salvation from disaster when they steer

Us clear, by text or email, from the sort
Of trouble we've got into when the talk
Goes wrong. Then all our good intent seems caught

In some perverse compulsion we can't chalk
Up to experience until we're taught
At last, prosthetically, to walk the walk
On networks that won't bring us up far short
Of home through natural tendency to fork

Off without warning into regions flagged
'Danger ahead'. Thus broadband brings the means
To stop those words of ours from getting snagged
By all the speech-mishaps that conjure scenes
Of chaos come again.
                So if it sagged,
Or seemed to, that mute converse of your genes
And his across the distance custom tagged
Uncrossable let's rather switch routines,

Take Hedy's lead, and tell ourselves instead
How fine, in truth, the line that separates
All selves and others, you and I, those bred
Up to conceive of human-only traits
As our pure essence and those firmly wed
To a bald naturalism that narrates
The tale from Darwin and takes it as read
That no such human essence correlates

With what's beyond all serious doubt revealed
By our best knowledge. I derive from this,
Along with other lessons from her field
Of second choice, the thought that we shall miss
Our last, best chance of knowing what's concealed
Within the maybe crossable abyss
Between divergent life-worlds if we wield

The sceptic's ancient privilege and kiss
Goodbye to the idea of a domain
Where, even though – or just because – it's shut,
As Blake and other mystics might maintain,
To our poor senses five, still there's a glut
Of other information that our brain
(Let's not resort to talk of soul or gut)
Has its own ways to process.
                              This makes plain
How finding sloth-talk nonsense tends to cut

Out fully nine tenths of what constitutes
Our world as habitable by the sorts
Of creature, like ourselves, whom it best suits
And, more than that, whom everything exhorts –
All creaturely and human attributes –
Not to give in when species-difference thwarts
Our overtures. Let's grant that this refutes
The confident sloth-whisperer who purports

To shrink that distance to the point where it's
A matter simply of their tuning in
To Sloth FM and tuning out the blitz
Of static or the message-scrambling din
That rules when Radio Anthropos transmits
Its all-subduing call for law of kin
To override whatever else befits
Us fellow-creatures, sloth or hominin,

For fellowship. No point pretending that's
All it involves, some voluntary switch
Of world-views or of psychic habitats

That lets us jump the species-gap and ditch
Our basic forms of life like acrobats
Defying gravity.
                    Hence the odd glitch
Or even (if we heed their caveats)
Those large-scale miscommunications which

The linguists and ethnologists so prize
As giving them a splendid chance to rub
Our noses in the sense-abyss that lies,
So far as we can know, right at the nub
Of every human bid to fraternize
By verbal means. Small chance, then, for those sub-
(Or supra-)verbal efforts to surmise
How else one might construe the seeming snub

Delivered, say, despite your silent plea
For some small evidence that his world-scheme
Has room for you, by every sign that he,
The pendent sloth, has no desire to team
Up with that frantic creature he can see
Presuming to invade his tranquil dream
Of solitude and steal the magic key
To his benign yet border-sealed regime

Of letting-be.
                    Yet you believed, and I
Believe you, that some message got across
Between the two of you and might apply
To you and me (no doubt the hopeful gloss
I've had in mind all through) as we defy
The odds those sceptics place on any toss

Of dice by which we contact-hopers try
To beat the odds. Worth risking some small loss

Of face if there's a chance we might, us two
Chance-coupled conspecifics, hitch a lift
On Hedy's neat idea for making do
With all those crowded airwaves that so miffed
The channel-fixers trusting to get through
On their set frequency. Go with the drift,
It says, till there may come, out of the blue,
A long-awaited momentary shift

Of signal strength that shows it's meant for you,
And you alone, without the need to sift
Or search for some authenticating clue
To source and sender. That's the way he sniffed
You out, I guess, sloth-fashion while I drew
Fresh courage from reflecting how your swift
Response to that trans-species rendezvous
Might count my life-world well within its gift.

DYLANELLE: THE GROUCHO VIEW

People are like stained-glass windows. They sparkle and shine when the sun is out, but when the darkness sets in, their true beauty is revealed only if there is a light from within. (Elisabeth Kübler-Ross, *On Grief and Grieving*)

Instead of encountering a pool of reflective calm she found herself interviewing 'one of the angriest, most difficult people I have ever met' . . . . Kübler-Ross had entered the sixth and final stage of dyng: rage at God for NOT letting her die . . . . She could only rage against the 'staying' of the light. (Adam Mars-Jones, 'Chop, Chop, Chop', *The London Review of Books*, 21st January 2016, p. 8)

But, of course, the opposite is also true. (Groucho Marx)

Rage, rage against the staying of the light.
Let's not deny it: Dylan loved his Dad,
But let's admit that Groucho got it right.

The Groucho version: psych Dad up to fight
Death tooth and nail until things get too bad,
But then rage at the staying of the light.

His larger point: for every truth you cite
There's one, flat contrary, that makes you add
A mental note that Groucho got it right.

Then going gentle into that good night
May seem a kindlier way than going mad
With rage against the staying of the light.

Let's not blame Dr. Kübler-Ross, despite
The moribund suspecting they've been had.
Let's just admit that Groucho got it right.

Still, her late temper-tantrums do invite
The thought that Thomas Junior was a tad
Too keen to urge the staying of the light.

Quite likely Dad just hoped to expedite
The final scene and yearned to tell his lad
How that wise jest of Groucho got it right.

Perhaps his one plea, 'there on the sad height',
Was: spare me this, your conjuring of sad
Refrains from that dread staying of the light.

For maybe those same rhymes that winged the flight
Of Dylan's verse then spawned its myriad
Ways of repeating: Groucho got it right;
Rage, rage against the staying of the light.

AN ANCIENT QUARREL

> *There is an ancient quarrel between philosophy and poetry, of which there are many proofs, such as the saying of "the yelping hound howling at her lord," or of one "mighty in the vain talk of fools."...Notwithstanding this, let us assure our sweet friend and the sister arts of imitation that if she will only prove her title to exist in a well-ordered State we shall be delighted to receive her—we are very conscious of her charms; but we may not on that account betray the truth.*

> —*Plato,* The Republic, *Book X*

Reader, beware: this poem has designs
    On you, your thinking, everything you take
As read when you proceed along the lines
    Laid down by truth and logic. It can make
No sense at all if intellect confines
    Its blessing to those texts that never shake
Thought's empire in a way that undermines
    Linguistic order merely for the sake

Of rhyme and meter. Metaphors condense
    Some dubious proposition, while the sound
Is not so much "an echo to the sense"
    As what permits verse-music to confound
All governance of reason or dispense
    With logic till the fallacies abound,

Tropes multiply in error's self-defence,
    And so we finish up with Ezra Pound

Still ranting in his cage. Let's not deny
    The evidence: take Eliot, Pound and Yeats,
Plus poet Lawrence, then consider why
    The life-and-times stuff always complicates
The issue at some crucial point whereby
    Their ranking with the literary greats
Strikes us as somehow ethically awry
    Unless indeed the poet's mind creates,

As Eliot said, works that should bear no trace
    Of the mere human being whose travails
Were their apparent theme. What if the case
    Looks bad for those high modernists, yet fails
To generalise? Just take another base-
    Line choice of poets and you'll find the scales
May tip the other way if those you place
    As counterweights are not (let's say) all males

With sexual hang-ups, all completely sold
    On fascist politics, or all crack-brained
Enough to need some mythic scheme to hold
    Their art and life together. Yet what's gained
By this defensive move, if truth be told,
    Makes no great odds against the old, deep-grained
Mistrust that's kept the boundaries patrolled
    From Plato down and zealously contained

Rhyme's threat to reason safely on the side
    Of lies or nonsense. Poetry they deem

Unfit to warrant reason's bona fide
   Enforced by sundry variants on the theme
Of "logic rules," in which case woe betide
   The poets, sophists, and their suspect team
Of word-artificers. Though they replied,
   That other lot, with boosts of self-esteem

Renaissance or Romantic in their style
   Of counter-claim, the old charge never quite
Lost its presumptive right to put on trial
   Whatever seeming truths the poet might
Rhapsodically convey and so beguile
   The reader as to win assent despite
Their better judgment. Thus the logophile
   Is torn both ways, between the sovereign right

Of *logos*—that of reason as the one
   And only self-legitimizing source
Of truthful speech—and all the *logoi* spun
   By word-spell weaving poets in the course
Of that old logomachia once begun
   By Plato *versus* Homer. So the force
Of dialectic's marshalled first to stun
   Its rival, then impose the strict divorce

That kept the *logos* properly apart
   From all those errant word-games that betrayed
The tricksy essence of the poet's art
   As simply what allowed them to persuade
The credulous and bid them take to heart
   Some pseudo-truth or argument gainsaid

By a mere moment's thought. Yet here we'll start,
    Perhaps, to wonder if the points thus made

In reason's cause by reason's favoured sorts
    Of argument, especially points scored
At poetry's expense, might signal thought's
    Old hedgehog tendency to take on board
Whatever prickly strategy purports
    To keep it safely curled up and afford
Protection when some metaphor distorts
    The proper sense of things. What they ignored,

Those hard-line literalists, was that which lay
    Within the poets' gift and might require
The kind of impropriety that they
    Turned to advantage, yet with no such dire
Mind-blowing consequences as dismay
    The heirs of Plato whose own texts aspire
To a plain style whereby to keep at bay
    Poetic language-games. Else these might fire

Strange passions of the kind that Plato kept,
    Or tried to keep, beneath prosaic wraps
Yet hidden in plain view because they leapt
    Off every page in metaphors or gaps
Of reasoning. The heirs find these inept
    Or blame them on some momentary lapse
From logic's rule while poet-types accept
    That they're the sort of word-event that taps

Into some language-region quite unknown
    To the plain-sense brigade, or into some

As yet unregimented meaning-zone
  Where echoes of an ancient quarrel come
Once more to haunt our thoughts. "What must be shown,
  Not said" would surely strike the *logos* dumb,
According to Saint Ludwig, though his own
  Vast *Nachlass* might suggest he failed to plumb

Such silent depths. The issue takes a whole
  New spin when Socrates, near death, avows
That poetry and music charm the soul
  More deeply than philosophy allows,
That maybe logic's steely thought-control
  Has failed him, and that therefore he'll espouse,
In his short time remaining, the new role
  Of one whom flute and poem can arouse

To heights of ecstasy unglimpsed by those,
  His former self among them, who'd decree
Such pleasures alien to the sober prose
  Of philosophic discourse. Here we see
What happens when one language-party goes
  Its own way, touts itself as master-key
To truth, and claims sole warrant to disclose
  All that's worth knowing to the devotee

Of that vocation. Poetry, and they'll
  Appeal to image, metaphor, and all
The ways that poems manage to unveil
  Truths that deliver us from logic's thrall;
Philosophy, and likely they'll avail
  Themselves of some device to reinstall

Sound logic as thought's organon and fail-
    Safe method for ensuring one not fall

Into some latest version of the same
    Linguistic-logical confusions that,
Conversely, guaranteed one's language-game
    Turn out nonsensical. Applied off pat
By partisans each creed distributes blame
    And praise by harking back to the old spat
Billed "Plato *versus* Homer" in the name
    Of some high calling destined to fall flat

On the sharp ears of those whose temperament
    Found ample room not only for the kinds
Of intellectual stimulus that went
    With exercise of thought for agile minds
But also for how how poets may invent
    New ways to see beyond whatever blinds
The stubborn literalist or represent
    New worlds beyond the habitude that binds

Our dulled perception to the fixed routine
    Of common usage. Yet it's still a touch
Too pat, too neat, let's say, too squeaky-clean
    As well as sub-Hegelian if such
A happy settling for the in-between
    Of those twin poles becomes a straw to clutch
Hopefully at for poet-thinkers keen
    That their allegiance seem not over-much

Committed either way. Perhaps we'd best
    Be less accommodating, more up-front

Or confrontational if we're to test
  The poet's claim to truth and not just shunt
That issue off into a siding lest
  Those gibes of Plato turn into such blunt
And heavy instruments that, in the quest
  For virtue, poetry should bear the brunt

Of every charge that reason ever brought
  Against its foes. They ranged from those it cast
As idiots or muddle-heads untaught
  In logic's ways to those it roundly classed
As gross corruptors of the laws of thought
  And hence—the jury verdict goes—as past
All hope of somehow learning to comport
  Themselves with more sagacity at last

Once freed from the delusion that led Keats,
  Absurdly, to promote "beauty is truth,
Truth beauty" as a formula that meets
  Truth's minimal demands, or take such sooth-
Saying twaddle as a dictum that defeats
  The cold abstractions of the logic-sleuth
By mere word-magic. Yet if this one cheats
  The reader by implying "how uncouth

To raise such logic-chopping points when there's
  So much of truth and beauty to be had
From heartfelt paradox," the question bears
  More pondering when to Keats's lines you add
Celan's rebuke to anyone who errs
  So far as to metaphorize the bad

Reality that hits us unawares
　　Through facts and dates that leave the reader glad

To find a refuge in the usual view
　　Of poetry as handily dispensed
From rules of plain truth-telling. So if you
　　Take them as less-than-literal or ring-fenced,
Those passages, by dint of some taboo
　　On facts in poems you'll run up against
His imagery of smoke or ash as true
　　In the most metaphorically condensed

Yet brute or plain-prose sense. Else you'll have failed
　　Celan's first test of readers well equipped
To cope with everything that so assailed
　　His memory that he must needs encrypt
Its import not in some discreetly veiled
　　Symbolic sense but rather in a script
Whose chiaroscuro characters entailed
　　A more prosaic reading duly stripped

Of all such poetry as might distract
　　Attention from whatever served to fix
His literal intent. Plain statement backed
　　By abstinence from anything that ticks
The 'poet' box would, so he thought, bring fact
　　Back with a vengeance and so knock for six
Those figural contrivances that lacked
　　The will to leave behind the bag of tricks

Called "poetry." Let exegetes refrain
　　From their old pact with poets of a more

Compliant character whose usual strain
   Of symbol, allegory, or metaphor
Gives ample scope for comment in a vein
   Accordant with the freedom to explore
New ways and means of finding some arcane
   Significance. This led them to ignore

Such details as would tend, if taken straight
   Or strictly *à la lettre*, to exceed
In power of utterance all that we equate,
   Us adepts of evasion, with the need
That metaphor provide a buffer-state
   Between ourselves and things of which we read
In its glass darkly so as to negate
   The shock of that which otherwise would feed

Our darkest terrors. Evidence enough,
   You might think, for the prosecution line
That has a poet like Celan say "Stuff
   Your poetry," or anyway define
His purpose as one long attempt to slough
   Off all that preciousness and re-assign
The poet's role as not just acting tough,
   Like vandals set to ruin culture's shrine,

Or speaking truth to power (though that's no doubt
   A large part of it), but as what insists
On writing things down literally without
   The verbal detours or the tropic twists
That once permitted poetry to flout
   All the fine protocols that truth enlists
On its side of this immemorial bout
   Of *Denker* versus *Dichter*. Though bare fists

Have now been pocketed we'd better grant
    One point to those of Plato's heirs for whom
"Poetic truth" remains a phrase they can't
    But find oxymoronic. If there's room
In poetry for sayings that enchant
    And elevate, still we should not presume
Too readily that some alternate slant
    On kindred themes won't conjure thoughts that loom

Uncomfortably large across the long
    And still unfolding history of wars
Provoked and waged through poetry and song
    From Homer down. There's no crusade or cause
So bad that bards won't answer like a gong
    Or put their tender consciences on pause,
Extol the right and castigate the wrong
    As if vouchsafed to them alone by laws

Of natural justice allied to the gift
    For moral divination that ensures
They judge aright when others go adrift.
    Yet it's just this self-certainty that lures
Them way off-course, like modernists who sniffed
    At all proposals save their drastic cures
For Europe's malady and gave short shrift
    To wiser, more pacific overtures

Of truth to power that grasped at neither horn
    Of the old fake dilemma. This demands
"Under which king, Bezonian?," holds in scorn
    All thought of compromise, and understands
By "truth" a mode of discourse either shorn

Of metaphor or such that it expands
To fill all history with fictions born
    In those mytho-poetic hinterlands

Where Yeatsian portents of apocalypse
    And Pound's cage-rattling Rapallo tirades
Still echo. So imagination tips
    Too quickly into conjuring the shades
Of ancient warriors or running clips
    From epic movies till the war-brigades
Recall some face that launched a thousand ships
    And once again its poetry invades

Mind, heart and culture. Then the poet's job
    Is clear enough: keep stoking the old fires,
Rework those tropes that mobilised the mob,
    Devize whatever myths the age requires,
And be prepared once in a while to lob
    A metaphoric bombshell that inspires
The arty types unwilling to hob-knob
    With those whose truth-preservative desires

Encourage a more literalist approach
    To any narrative of war and its
Brute consequences. These require we broach
    The matter in a way that closely fits

The factual evidence lest myth encroach
    On history by deleting all the bits
That don't so fit and making sure to coach
    Its adepts with the self-assembly kits

In fiction's user-guide. That says: though *res*
   Gestae should not be mixed up with *historia*
Rerum gestarum, still the many ways
   Of plot-construction—from *sic transit gloria*
To Whiggish narratives—suggest it pays
   To shop around in various emporia,
Peruse the range of story-lines, and raise
   The joint claim of *poiesis* and *theoria*

To new-found heights. Then it may well forego
   That quaint idea of segregating what
Old-style *historia* takes itself to know
   On factual warrant arduously got
By long research and what its methods owe
   To all the deft contrivances of plot
And discourse. Hence the shrewdly managed flow
   Of narrative events that shows we're not

Here in the hands of a historian whose
   First obligation is to get things right
On Clio's terms, but one for whom the muse
   Of poetry requires that they should write
Such tales as a skilled dramatist might choose
   So as first to astonish, then delight
(A classic formula) and thus infuse,
   In good Horatian style, some pleasing flight

Of fancy into history's bitter pill
   Of factual discipline. Yet who'll deny
The counter-claim: that some war-poets' skill
   In verse-technique or plentiful supply
Of metaphor can't hide the strength of will

It took to get those poems out and vie
With other poets' efforts to instil
  A jingo-creed. This prompted some to die

Like cattle, and the others first to kill
  Then die like prize-bulls led to slaughter by
The far from un-poetic power to thrill
  Responsive temperaments in those whose high-
Toned rhetoric promised swiftly to fulfil
  Their inchoate desires. Although we try,
Like this, to sort poetic good from ill
  As if the crucial difference must lie

In some marked feature that the standard drill
  Of Eng Lit Crit should help us to descry
With reasonable accuracy, still
  The case is apt to baffle or defy
(As here) our need to answer it until,
  As theories fail, we're left to satisfy
The need for grist to our vexatious mill
  With poems no high tone can overfly.

A BROKEN MUSIC

This poem has to do with the disputed place of rhyme and meter in a literary culture routinely doubtful of their continuing claims on the serious attention of anyone alive to the poetic *Zeitgeist*. It reflects on the uses of off-rhyme, half-rhyme, quasi-rhyme and their sundry relatives in the poetry of anti-war "war poets" like Wilfred Owen and Siegfried Sassoon, and suggests—argues!—that rhyme and metre are resources that poetry had better hang on to in however pointedly deviant or off-key a form. The last few stanzas give the briefest of airings to my notion that the turn against them in poetry has a good deal in common with the proclaimed obsolescence of tonality as urged in the more dogmatic quarters of post-Schoenberg musical modernism. On my own principles there shouldn't be too much difference—certainly not a logic-bending or argument-slackening difference—between getting a case to work out cogently in prose and getting it to work out persuasively in verse. Still there had better be enough difference in the way the two things are done for the verse to count as poetry for at least some of the time.

"A Broken Music" rather pushes its luck in that respect, not least—in what I'd like to call a piece of large-scale structural irony—by using perfect rather than off- or half-rhymes throughout. This goes, albeit obliquely, to underline the poem's point: that the latter devices work best (are most strongly motivated and justified) in contexts of extreme conflict, stress, or emotional pressure like that of Owen's war poetry.

Sassoon and Owen told it like it was.
  None of your fine uplifting stuff for those
Who'd been there, seen the worst, and then—because
  Of what they'd seen—wrenched language to expose

The old lie these two nailed. Stuff your applause,
     Their off-rhymes said, for the false art that goes
Into a well-bred verse-technique and draws
     High praise for its devices to keep prose,

Along with factual reportage, at bay,
     So showing its rapt readership (by grace
Of flawless rhyme and meter) the best way
     To gain safe entrance to the other place,
That tranquil "corner of some foreign field." Here they
     Can act out their heroics in a space
Reserved for poetasters who obey,
     Like him, the rule: let prosody outface

All such threats to its sacrosanct domain
     As might come from a poetry that veers
Rhyme-wise and metrically against the grain,
     As also from the moral shift of gears
Whereby those two condemned the whole insane
     Scenario where escalating fears
On both sides conjured up the very bane
     Both sides made war on. For indeed the spheres

Where warmongers and lyric warblers dwell
     Are not so far apart as might be thought
Since, after all, the stories both lots tell
     By popular request are of the sort
That help conceal whatever glimpse of hell
     Might otherwise poke through and so cut short
Those stirring tales with accents that rebel
     Against the martial beat. If they distort
The victor's view of things it's by the kind

Of dislocating jolt that shocks the old-
School prosodists as much as those who find
    The devil's hand in all that breaks the mould
Of custom or explodes the lies that bind
    Bad poets to bad causes. These take hold
Through formulas that line us up behind
    Their source in myths or meters tight-controlled

By emanations of the Nietzschean Will-
    To-Power whose long dissimulated drive
Adopts more subtly muted forms until
    It spawns those calls-to-slaughter that contrive
To sound like elegies, or tales that thrill
    The warrior nerve yet whose narrators strive
To couch them in such tones as might instil
    No craving more malign than to revive

Time-honoured pieties. We may expect
    This age-old ruse itself to undergo
Revivals on the principle that Brecht
    Spelled out with grim precision: that although
They'd stood up, killed the bastard, and so checked
    One Hitler in his tracks, still they should know
That all their hopes of progress might be wrecked
    The next time round. Brecht's closing comments go

More snappily: that even now "the bitch
    That bore him is in heat again," so they'd
Best not allow this latest hard-won switch
    Of fortunes to annul the gains they'd made
By letting false assurances bewitch

Their wiser minds. That's roughly what's conveyed
By Owen's off-key rhymes that queer the pitch
  For anyone whose aural nerves are frayed

When poets heed Brecht's lesson and refuse
  The Brookean way of melding perfect rhymes
With classic verse-forms. It's a mode that woos
  The unresisting reader and so primes
The violence masked by all those strict taboos
  That bid state-chroniclers ignore state-crimes
Or teach tame versifiers how to schmooze
  The regnant powers by any style that chimes

With regnant tastes. Yet Brecht's point still applies
  When free-verse zealots tout a final break
With rhyme and meter since they'd otherwise
  (They think) be fobbing readers off with fake
Emotions like the old-time poet guys
  Who wrote such stuff. In which case better take
The creed on board full-strength and improvise,
  Like true verse-liberators, ways to make

 A virtue of relinquishing control
  And, above all, not adding to the pile
Of well-formed verbal icons. So the sole
  Constraint you'll need to have in mind—since style
Comes down to what permits an easy stroll
  Through genial themes—is how best to beguile
The passive reader who's assigned a role
  With no allowance for such versatile

Capacities as once required a keen
　　And practised ear. Such were the skills that went
Into that amicable strife between
　　Speech-rhythms and how meter would accent
The poet's vocables had they not been
　　Still part-immersed within the element
Of ordinary speech that had them mean,
　　Up to a point, what those words would have meant

In plain-prose talk. Yet—some would say—beyond
　　That point the poem enters realms unknown
To all save some few readers who respond
　　In ways that verbal acumen alone
Could scarcely grasp. At least they won't be conned,
　　Those *vers-libristes*, by any jumped-up tone
That strives to transcendentalize the bond
　　Of sound and sense, so leaving sceptics prone

To seek salvation in a cult of free-
　　Form verse that yokes its star to the eclipse
Of formal structure since its apogee
　　Comes often when a martial fervour grips
The poets and induces them to see
　　No merit but in poetry that whips
Up kindred sentiments. For them, the key
　　To truth in verse is that which promptly tips

The reader off that here we have a case
　　Of skilled technique so splendidly at one
With its high theme that every verbal grace
　　Conspires to spin the yarn routinely spun

By poets keen to show their public face
    To best advantage through a lengthy run
Of formal features perfectly in place.
    Whence their late-comers' stake in work begun

In that primordial tryst of sound and sense
    Through which, as Benjamin obscurely said,
Adam once had the genius to condense
    Kind-fixing essences in names that led
Him, first and last among us, to dispense
    With *l'arbitraire du signe* and instead
Bestow God's signatures. Thus would commence
    The poets' endless quest for what might wed

Sound, sense and reference in a union blessed
    By the old Cratylist belief that signs
Might once again reveal themselves possessed
    Of such Adamic power. When this combines
With lyric feelings of the sort expressed
    In (let's admit) the most effective lines
From Brooke's Grantchester poem—like the rest
    Of those whose martial character defines

"War poetry" pre-Owen and Sassoon,
    And all too often since—the mixture's apt
To stir emotions through an opportune
    Deployment of the language-functions mapped
By formalists as an almighty boon
    To poets and recruiting-sergeants wrapped
In words like flags. That's why the more rough-hewn
    Verse-forms and rhythms nowadays adapt

So readily to what the ear perceives
   As beauty's crying need to give the beast
Its chance, or anyway be sure it leaves
   Some space where verse-disorder can at least
Find elbow-room. That's also why what "heaves
   The heart into the mouth"—what old Lear ceased
To credit far too late—is that which weaves
   A story-line whose mob-appeal's increased

Ten-fold by those well-practised verse techniques
   Which prompt the disaffected to resist
Their suasive force by all the Brechtian tweaks
   Of formal structure that contrive to twist
The sense around and skew whatever seeks
   To reinforce the customary gist
Of martial oratory with verse that speaks
   Only those noble lies that serve as grist

To some warmonger's mill. And yet, and yet,
   How should we hope to figure out what's true
In poetry, or even—just to let
   The Larkin qualifier have its due—
Not wholly untrue, if the meter's set
   At zero deviance from what will do
In daily chatter? Then it's a safe bet
   That, since such attributes are now taboo,

All remnant rhymes or half-rhymes will be held
   Just chance events, or put down to some sad
Since past-fixated practice, or expelled
   From poet-school as witnessing a bad
Since rhyme-fixated ear. Though they rebelled,

Those anti-prosodists, against what had
By then such false allure as might have quelled
　　Those poets' songs at source or sent them mad

Through formal servitude, still they'd have hit
　　A truer key-note if they'd picked the route
That led to Owen's off-rhymes as the grit
　　In his best pearls, or chosen to permute
The rhyme-rules so as each time to commit
　　A well-judged breach of concord and so suit
Medium to message in an age unfit
　　For ampler harmonies. Let's not impute

Some failure of poetic nerve or lapse
　　Into false consciousness should poets opt
To use verse-forms that, though they may set traps
　　For less attentive readers, might have stopped
Those readers, plus some poets—Brooke perhaps—
　　From doing war-work elegantly propped
By classic rhyme and meter. If this taps
　　A formal drive we moderns should have swapped

For manners less amenable, that's not
　　To play Cassandra to the greatest gift
That rhyme and meter bring with them, like plot
　　In fiction, one that promises to lift
The curse of mythic claims to know the lot
　　Back to year zero then down through each shift
In Being's tone. Rather, they help us spot
　　The sorts of claim where Being is likelier miffed

At such portentous talk but also those
    Where an off-rhyme or rhythmic twist athwart
The metric pulse conveys to one who knows
    How poems work that this must be the sort
Of verse, like Owen's, to help diagnose
    What shock first cracked rhyme's bell were we but taught
Such hermeneutic tact as might disclose
    Where things went wrong. The lessons here, in short:

Watch out when rhyme's seduction starts to lead
    The mind on etymo-poetic tracks
Since that's where (*vide* Heidegger) there breed
    Monsters in plenty. Still we should relax
The veto just so far as to concede
    How verse-forms might not merely fill the cracks
In culture's edifice but meet a need
    Unmet by any poetry that lacks

A sense of rhyme's beneficence or feel
    For meter's gift to thought. Else it's as if
We took the Schoenberg line as a done deal,
    Made a fixed rule of his high-profile tiff
With tonal harmony, and set our seal
    Of musical approval on no riff
Or note-row that betrayed a flagging zeal
    For atonality. So there's a whiff

Of self-denying ordinance or sheer
    Perversity about the drive against
Those formal features that, *vers-libristes* fear,
    Will leave the realm of poetry so fenced
Around with props and outworks that to clear

Them off's the Sisyphean task commenced
Each time from scratch by those at the frontier
   Where art has to negotiate its tensed

Encounter with Apollo. Thus what tends
   To shield it from exposure to the "air
Of a new planet" (Schoenberg) and so lends
   Fresh courage to the tribe of *derrière-*
Gardistes is just what sundry later trends
   Of free verse helped to propagate since they're
Intent on smoothing out all that offends
   A cautious ear and mind whose only care

Is not to interact in risky ways
   That might expose their partnership to some
Full-scale *dérèglement*. It's here rhyme plays
   Its duplex role through sound-effects that come
Most often as the tribute music pays
   To speech in a well-tuned sensorium
But sometimes, as in Owen, out-of-phase
   With any vibes remotely tuned to drum

Up sentiments in that heroic vein
   That Plato said defined the only mode
Of music fit to hear. The vocal grain
   Of rhyme, once brushed against, may then encode
Resistance to the grand-heroic strain
   Of thought or feeling with a force that's owed
To its still pitching camp on rhyme's terrain
   Now mined with off-rhymes ready to explode.

By this stage, reader, you'll be quick to catch
    Me out in having taken pains to rhyme
Ear-charmingly, and making sure to match
    Speech-stress with metric pulse, while all the time
Admonishing that poets not attach
    Such weight to mere effects of verbal chime
Or fluent verse-technique. Let me dispatch
    That point with this *tu quoque*: think what I'm

Essaying here, then think of what they did
    In verse, the Owens and Sassoons, to stave
Off horrors such that pity might forbid
    Some Dante *redivivus* to engrave
Their truth in words that opened wide the lid
    On sufferings worse than even God could crave,
That stoker of infernos. It's the *quid*
    Pro quo of verse-redemption that they save,

Those poets, from co-option by the force
    Of habit, usage, rhythm, rhyme, or all
Thought-regimens that coax us to endorse
    The way things are. These readily enthral
Our morals, like our language, to some source
    Of wisdom or authority on call
When needed since, with custom's late divorce
    From conscience, every case is apt to fall

Under some code or other. So it's crass
    (Forgive me, reader) to suppose my verse
Must risk a flat performative impasse
    Should it flunk Conrad's dictum to "immerse
In the destructive element," amass

The bitter truths accrued from Adam's curse
To Auden's "history may say alas,"
    And through *discordia concors* then disburse

Scant reparation. Hence the tribute paid
    By Owen's *ars poetica* to both
The savagery those clashing rhymes portrayed
    And the farewell to it ("My hands were loath
And cold"). Most likely a denouement they'd
    Reject, the pacifists, since it's the sloth
Of sheer war-weariness that's here displayed
    And not, as might be hoped, the heartfelt troth

Of one who finds "kill or be killed" at last
    A deathwatch maxim that indeed pertains,
Like Maxim guns, to a benighted past
    Or kingdom of the blind. That's why the strains
Show up in verse-forms not so much recast
    As wrenched to fit what little now remains
Of their old dignity and so hold fast,
    Despite the language-ravaging campaigns

Of neo-barbarism, to the chance
    That in such broken rhymes there might endure
Something of Psyche's strength to look askance
    At each new threat. What vanquishes the pure
In heart, bloodline or diction may enhance
    That strength and help such hybrid types ensure
Survival through the half-averted glance
    That joins with subtlest mindset to secure

Just the apotropaic power required
    To ward off swarming horrors from the sleep
Of reason. Better then it not get tired
    For lack of formal exercise to keep
On the *qui vive* against those long-expired
    Verse-genres now retailing on the cheap,
Yet also have its rhythmic nerve-ends fired
    And its imagination take a leap

Not just when subject to the usual sorts
    Of poet-prompt but at the kinds that bare
A nerve so raw that rhyme itself contorts
    Into strange couplings that may seem to share
No more with old ideas of what comports
    With what than we've good warrant to compare
Wars new and old. And so it self-aborts,
    Old rhyme, or else attempts to self-repair

Only to self-transform into a stun-
    Grenade with pin drawn ready to be thrown
Back in and finish any work undone
    In war's long harrowing of the border-zone
Where rhyme and reason merge. If, then, there's none
    Of that discordant music in my own
Traversal it's because this mother's son
    Wrote, thankfully, of things he'd never known.

DAYS

I tend to take the groundhog view of days,
   Those chronic revenants, but you,
My darling, wake most mornings and, before
   I've time to phrase
The self-fulfilling thought, undo
   Some catch that kept the door

Shut tight against all hopes that might erase
   The groundhog loop. For it's a new
Day, as you now remind me, and what's more
   (Such thoughts amaze
You as they should) a day of blue-
   Sky prospects yet in store

For all the multi-million different ways
   Our lives could always go to skew
Their routine compass-points. For then us shore-
   Bound types might raise
Long-downcast eyes to where the view
   Now bids them freely soar

And readjust their coast-accustomed gaze
   To oceans glimpsed 'not with but through
The eye', as Blake desired. Else we ignore
   All that the haze
Of habit had us misconstrue
   As simply down to poor

Eyesight or some such sensory malaise,
  So finding reason to eschew
That matutinal glory-song as your
  New trick to faze
The mind of a late-sleeper who,
  Like me, lies waiting for

A sub-ecstatic wake-up that delays
  The dawn assault. Way out of true,
I've come to think, the idea that would draw
  From that which stays
The flagging spirit just a few
  Stock pretexts to deplore

As mere credulity whatever pays,
  In just your way, the homage due
To days. For it's their dawnings underscore
  Each latest phase
Of our awakening that drew
  First light from night's rapport.

HYSTERON-PROTERON (DOUBLE SONNET)

I admit that I do not understand the title that Chopin liked to give these short pieces: Preludes. Preludes to what?

> —*André Gide, "Notes on Chopin"*

When Liszt wrote that "they are not only pieces destined to be played in the guise of introductions to other pieces," the key word is "only": Liszt at once admitted the traditional function of the genre while he praised the poetic ways in which Chopin's contribution exceeded this tradition.

> —*Jeffrey Kallberg,* Chopin at the Boundaries

It is but an hysteron proteron, and preposterous conceit, to fancie wages before the work . . .

> —*Henry More,* Annotations *(1682)*

What are these preludes preludes to?, asked Gide,
   Of Chopin as it happens, though he might
Have pressed the query further. What if he'd
   Opted to turn the thing around, re-write
The rule of part and whole, and ask instead
   By what generic warrant it should seem
Plain true to say, of anything we've read,
   Or thought, or said, that this exhausts the theme
Or ends the prelude? That which guaranteed

The law of genre never managed quite
To screen all mixed-mode variants that might lead
    Beyond its safe enclosure to a site
Of meanings, melodies, or forms ill-bred
    As breeding goes. This metaleptic scheme
For genre-stretching gives the go-ahead,
    Like double-sonnet form, to move upstream
Against the backward pull, yet not exceed
    The norm so far that then it seems alright
To skim-write or to aquaplane. What's freed
    From custom's grip or newly brought to light
By hybrid modes is all the things unsaid
    As much by those subdued to the regime
Of formal rectitude as those who tread
    Undaunted where the first lot fear to dream.
So Gide's enquiry begs us grant the need
    For lingering cadences that won't incite
The rage for closure in an ear misled
    By chords one false relation might redeem.

TERZA RIMA FOR TERRY
(MEANING BY HAWKES)[1]

Terry Hawkes was my mentor, colleague in Cardiff, good friend, and regular Saturday-night drinking companion for more than three decades, so his death in January 2014 left me wishing we had remained more closely in touch during the past few years. I had two main reasons for choosing what might seem the quaint or distinctly eighteenth-century genre of verse-essay or verse-epistle. One was our last exchange of emails when Terry had said some typically acute and generous things about previous ventures of mine in a similar mode. The second was my feeling that the style and ethos of that period were close to what Terry most enjoyed about living in the cross-over zone between academe, literary journalism, and critical theory where the gloves were apt to come off—at any rate in print—and a ready wit would often do vital service alongside critical acumen and depth of scholarship. He wouldn't have wanted solemn proceedings so I tried to evoke—rather than match or imitate—something of Terry's own cheerfully irreverent, unfailingly good-humored, verbally inventive, at times polemically hard-hitting but never less than genial and magnanimous spirit.

The main topic is of course "theory" and the large—indeed central—role he played in propagating new ideas about literature, criticism, and culture through his editorship, from the early 1980s on, of the *New Accents* book series and the journal *Textual Practice*. The poem also talks a lot about Terry's truly ground-breaking essays in Shakespeare criticism, his frequent run-ins with hostile (anti-theory) reviewers and respondents, and his expert deployment of cultural-materialist readings as a natural extension of adversarial class politics within and beyond the academy. These went along with his singular gift—or creative flair—for approaching issues of Shakespeare interpretation via some ingeniously reconstructed set of historical and/or personal circumstances as they bore on some particular scholar-critic at some especially salient or critical point in a play's reception-history. Terry's essay on Dover Wilson's notably over-determined relationship to "Hamlet" was (I think) the first of these exhilarating ventures and, for my money, the most inspirational, so it figures as the main point of reference here.

What the poem tries to do in a more general way is make the case that opponents of literary theory—some teachers of creative writing among them—are getting it wrong when they posit a kind of inbuilt antagonism between it and the processes, whatever these may be, involved in writing poetry or fiction. One way to challenge that idea is to point out how many students at various levels choose to do both and manage to combine them with no signs of stress or cognitive/creative dissonance. Another—more prominent here—is the sheer self-evidence of literary as well as intellectual creativity in a critic/theorist like Terry and others who looked to literary theory as offering a welcome release from the strictures of mainstream academic discourse. Debunking the more arrogant or self-serving claims of creative writers was undoubtedly one of Terry's favorite pastimes and very likely has something to do with the kinds of ambivalence or creative-critical tension—if not the full-scale Bloomian "anxiety"—plainly legible in critics like Geoffrey Hartman and the Yale acolytes of deconstruction. However in Terry's case the creativity expressed itself far more directly and with no such agonized quasi-Freudian detours, displacements, or sublimations. Scholarship and criticism were creative activities for him, and he did more than anyone since William Empson to show that writing about Shakespeare had better be criticism as "answerable style"—in Hartman's well-chosen phrase—if it was to have any claim on our receptive-responsive powers.

Anyway I hope that some of this will come across in the poem which I dedicate not only to Terry's memory but also to that other eminent Shakespearean, John Drakakis. John did more than anyone over the past thirty years both to carry on the cultural-materialist project and, after Terry's first major illness, to put him back in touch with his colleagues and admirers around the world.

The Cardiff thing it was, plus things that went
　　Much farther back—mum, dad, class stuff, and school,
In your case Handsworth Grammar, where they sent

Bright kids to learn the ropes in ways that you'll
    Soon learn to turn around against the bunch
Of snooty Oxbridge types. Nobody's fool

Unless, like Lear's, the one who had a hunch
    That speaking truth to power was something best
Done by convincing them you're out to lunch

On some wild anecdote or screwball jest
    Which then—before they notice it—turns out
A real game-changer. That was how you'd test

Those manor-born Shakespeareans who'd tout
    Their natural entitlement to tell
Us groundlings what the plays were all about,

Or how us dull provincials would do well
    To cultivate a decent reverence
For such transcendent genius. This should quell

All thought that common readers could dispense
    With mediation by the fit though few
Interpreters who'd properly make sense

Of things and help the hoi polloi construe
    What otherwise would surely stretch their poor
Resources past endurance. So when you

Came up with sundry items from the store
    Of odd Shakespeareana—all those tales
Retrieved from centuries of scholar-lore

Or followed back along the mazy trails
    Of critics' lives and times—it was to show
Bardolators what craziness prevails

When zealous champions of the status quo
    In Shakespeare studies, such as (let's recall)
J. Dover Wilson,[2] pledged themselves to go

That extra step in striving to forestall
    The least suggestion that in truth their god
Might sometimes err or even *Hamlet* fall

To Greg's critique.[3] Should its creator nod
    And it not hang together then (he wrote
In *Milestones on the Dover Road*) the squad

Of strikers up North might as well just vote
    To join the Soviets since, as well as Greg's
Outrageous article, he'd taken note

On his rail journey up to meet the dregs
    Of disaffected labor how the press
On that same day was putting all its eggs

In revolution's basket. Just to stress
    Him out yet further the war-effort now
Looked well-nigh certain to collapse unless

He won them over and contrived somehow,
    In this his current role, to get the strike-
Call lifted and persuade them to allow

Munitions through despite his strong dislike
    (Think Coriolanus) of the fawning role
This might require. You figured how he'd psych

Himself up and establish his control
    Over these looming crises by the choice,
From then on, more devoutly to extol

Great Shakespeare's genius, give that genius voice
    Through commentary, and so redeem its claim
Against all comers. Chiefly he'd rejoice

In giving back to *Hamlet* its good name
    Against the charge of playing fast and loose
With time-scales or enjoying unjust fame

Since the cracked plot gives Hamlet no excuse
    For his wild conduct.
                        Other critics caught
On soon enough and started to produce

More Shakespeare criticism of the sort
    You trail-blazed there, but didn't have the near-
Shakespearean dexterity of thought

Or—what enabled that—a poet's ear
    (There were some early poems, but you kept
The fact well hidden) for effects of sheer

Linguistic serendipity. These leapt,
    For you, right off the page or gave the cue
For jokes and puns unthinkable except

By way of those same language-paths that you,
    The signifier-sleuth, had tracked so far
Into Shakespearean country that the view

At times seemed quite *unheimlich*.[4] If we are,
    In truth, all these years on still just a touch
Bewildered maybe it's because the star

We hitched our lumbering wagons to was such
    A dazzler that it left the common sky
Of scholarship a zone where nothing much

Stood out compared with how some pure *trouvaille*,
    Some chance encounter turned up in the course
Of (maybe) casual reading, by and by

Took on the unlikely role of vaulting-horse
    To scenes, real or imagined, that supplied
Through Prospero-like conjuring a source

Of critical perspectives from outside
    The goldfish-bowl they'd made of academe,
Those keepers of the flame. That's why you tried

To get them off that old imperial theme,[5]
    To show them how the transcendental stuff
(Traversi and the like[6]) ran out of steam

Once recognized as just a high-toned puff
    For fascism, to *épater* the kind
Of Oxbridge tone you caught when Graham Hough[7]

Reviewed those first *New Accents* books ("please mind
   Your language—don't say that," they begged in vain,
Your publisher and everyone inclined

To smooth things over), and—surely a main
   Intent of all your work—to take a hint
From Marx, confront them on their own terrain,

The Eng Lit gentry, call them out in print,
   And give no quarter to the dozy heirs
Of scholar-privilege. To look asquint

At all the classic texts they took as theirs,
   As if by right, to annotate and gloss
Was your big strategy to kick upstairs

Your young "New Accents" crew and teach the boss-
   Class how their precious canon might emerge
Scrubbed up and sprightlier despite the loss

Of culture-capital. A very scourge,
   They thought, with new barbarians at the gate
And cultural materialists[8] set to purge

The libraries till no vestige of the Great
   Works they'd long served now lingered to reproach
Them for their failure to avert the fate

Of literature once theory drove a coach
   And horses through the delicate rapport
Of text and reader. Truth is, you could poach

The big game—even Shakespeare—right before
      The big game-keepers' eyes because you'd read
The plays more often, better, and with more

Attention to what other critics said,
      Or—just as relevantly—didn't say
But wrapped in secrecy, so that instead

It fell to you and those who knew a way
      Of making silence speak to unconceal
The interests that required they not betray

Such less than noble truths. You had a feel
      For just what hidden crux it was in this
Or that Shakespearean text that made them deal

With it so off-the-pointedly, or miss
      The mark with such persistence that their lapse
Of insight brought the hermeneutic kiss

Of life to those you'd helped to see the gaps
      In classic texts as not to be repaired
By some discreet re-drawing of the maps

To join them up. Rather it meant a shared
      Re-cultivation of the common land
Long since enclosed by critics who declared

Themselves uniquely fit to take a stand
      On matters that required the exercise
Of literary judgment, not the hand-

Me-down ideas that took the Theory prize
    (They liked to joke) for ways of passing off
Some half-baked notion in the splendid guise

Of some new jargon coined by some new prof
    At the Sorbonne, or Yale, or any place
Except (as Leavisites were prone to scoff⁹)

The kinds of native habitat by grace
    Of which the star-struck theorists might have learned
That well-trained readers didn't need to chase

After strange gods. Such jibes you shrewdly turned
    Around and batted back with perfect ease,
So that *New Accents*-bashers always earned

Not just another point-by-point reprise
    Of where they'd got it wrong but, lest they not
Quite cotton on, a joke or two to tease

Them into seeing how they'd lost the plot,
    Whether in reading Shakespeare or *That Shakes*
Peherian Rag, because of some blind-spot

Or (more like) ear that's deaf to what it takes
    To write engagingly about a text
Whose challenge to the keen-eared critic makes

That task the more demanding. This perplexed
    Those on the anti-theory side who took
For granted how the curse of theory hexed

Our language-sense, although the merest look
  At any page of yours would quickly serve
To knock that thought for six and cock a snook

At all those cloth-eared types who had the nerve
  To set aside the awkward truth that yours,
Not theirs, is writing with the kind of verve

And creativity that's on all fours
  With how good poets (Shakespeare more than most)
Took every verbal chance to settle scores

With proto-puritans whose proudest boast,
  Back then as now, was to make doubly sure
That errant thought not conjure up a coast

For its Bohemia[10] and thereby secure
  Full-scale poetic license.
                  There are some
Of your late essays where the marsh-light lure

Of wordplay—as, by Johnson's time,[11] they'd come
  To think it—largely frees you from the rules
Of normal scholarship and lets you drum

Out syncopated readings where old tools
  Won't fill the bill since it's your jazz-inspired
Prosodic and thematic riffs when school's

Out, so to speak, that kept your prose live-wired
  And keeps the circuits humming when we read
You now. Most likely the same neurons fired

Each time an agent rang to say they'd need
 A trad-style drummer up to handling things
When some jazz legend came to town. Then we'd

Just happen by and think how your prose swings
 The accent phrase to phrase yet always keeps
In view the cunning denouement that springs

A shocker such as positively leaps
 To eye (take Armstrong/Fortinbras![12]) once sprung
But, on a first encounter, either sweeps

All scruples clean aside or seems far-flung,
 Like Shakespeare's puns to Johnson, way beyond
What mutual interests and a common tongue

Required to keep intact the vital bond
 Of civil concord. You had little use
For suchlike notions, thinking them *au fond*

Just means to reinforce or reproduce
 The same old deferential ways of talk
That education plus a bit of nous

Should get us over once we've learned to chalk
 Up every stage along the post-war road
As either one step in the lengthy walk

To social justice, since it breaks the code
 Of class-respect, or else a backward lurch
Since, like unthinking reverence bestowed

By rote on classic texts, it makes a church
    Where orthodoxy's prized at the expense
Of thought. Let's call your project not "research"—

A word you loathed, along with "excellence,"
    "Engagement," "impact," "added value," plus
"Empower" and "innovate"—but more a sense

Of what might do best service with least fuss
    To show those culture-rituals up as mere
"Keep off the classics" notices for us

"*New Accents*" types who'd best not interfere
    With matters that lay properly within
An altogether more exalted sphere

Of judgment. These include—lest we begin,
    Thus theory-primed, to get ideas above
Our station—asking why the critics pin

Transcendent value to the sorts of love-
    Intrigue that leave straight gender-roles intact,
Or why that preference goes hand-in-glove

With others, such as choosing who gets backed
    For all the fellowships, or qualifies
As "research-active" owing to the fact

Of having come up publication-wise
    With stuff in the right places.
                        There are those—
And were from early on—who say: "You guys,

The theorists, were the first ones to impose
    This periodic curse, the latest round
Of research-auditing, since you first chose

To publish all those theory-books they found
    Offensive, no doubt, but a ready-made
Excuse for telling everyone they're bound

Contractually to keep up the cascade
    Of four-star items or resign themselves
Either to have some bureaucrat degrade

Their post to 'teaching only,' or stack shelves
    In Tesco." More than that, the charge-sheet runs
To saying that the theory-stuff just delves

A little distance down so we're the ones,
    Us early converts, who kicked off the whole
Bad shooting-match by turning round the guns

Of critical dissent against the sole
    Resource that might just possibly avail
To dig us theorists out of this deep hole

We'd dug ourselves. Best reassess our scale
    Of values so as not to let the drive
For theory-centered projects so assail

Our judgment that no thoughts of ours survive
    Beyond the stage of critical review
By some internal censor set to strive

For maximum research-points with as few
　　Hours spent in gaining them as might be spared
From writing research-grant proposals. You

Were quick to say, whenever someone aired
　　This anti-theory charge, that what they missed
By such comparisons was just what scared

Both management and those recidivist
　　Upholders of the canon whose real gripe
With each new book on the "*New Accents*" list

Involved their sense that talents of the type
　　That went to make good theorists also went
To make the sorts of literature they'd hype,

Those canonists, as fit to represent
　　The human mind at full creative stretch.
Yet then it seemed the speculative bent

Of theory worked, like poetry, to fetch
　　Up thoughts, ideas, and images unknown
To those who gave the standard hostile sketch

Of its agenda in the standard tone
　　Of high disdain. Your writing had a gift
For skewering those reviewers (all the clone-

Like Leavisites especially) who'd lift
　　Their pen as if reluctantly compelled
To set you straight, then show themselves adrift

Or floundering when it came to concepts spelled
　　Out as who runs may read in your precise,
Well-groomed, yet laid-back style that so excelled

In knowing just what joke might best suffice
　　To make the point.
　　　　　　　　　So really what we need's
Not some routine infusion of cut-price

Arnoldian high seriousness that bleeds
　　Away into low posturing as soon
As tried, but more an attitude that heeds

Your "Twenty Hamlets" point[13]: let's take the tune,
　　The basic theme, then run as many riffs
On it as some jazz vocalist might croon

Or Shakespeare critic spin against the ifs-
　　And-buts platoon of scholars set to wage
Their old campaign anew through endless tiffs

In *Notes & Queries*. Sounding off with sage
　　Remarks, like Leavis, on the sorry state
Of things would get a laugh on Shakespeare's stage,

Or catcalls, or be heard at any rate
　　As just the kind of talk that malcontents
Will typically come on and use to bait

A restive audience. Take their two cents'
　　Worth, you'd advise, but see the other side,
Their comic aspect, since it best prevents

The sorts of finger-wagging talk you tried
    To show was just as out-of-place when used
By jazz-authenticists as when applied

By high-toned Shakespeare critics who accused
    You and your rebel crew of making light
Those themes that, weighed more carefully, refused

Such infra-dig recension. Yet despite
    That Brechtian or Bakhtinian readiness
To thumb your nose[14] whenever you caught sight

Of pious posturing (the TLS
    Once ran a photo of you and referred
To your coiffure, and maybe style of dress,

As "a poor man's Jacques Derrida") you heard
    Far subtler nuances and finer shades
Of meaning in some long neglected word

Than ever struck the not-so-light brigades
    Of Shakespeare savants. They deplored the *lèse-*
Majesté of a writing that degrades,

So they suppose, the solemn offices
    Of scholarship—here taking the same line
As, long ago, l'Académie Française

On Shakespeare—yet in truth's a very mine
    Of senses lost on those with filters set
To block whatever readings they'd incline

To count as signs of how absurd things get
    When presentism bids our better part[15]
Of judgment screw itself. For then we let

Anachronistic fancy trump the art
    Of balancing (they say) a due respect
For what's been made of Shakespeare's works by smart

Interpreters against—lest we neglect
    The scholar-critic's calling—a robust
Sense of how texts, like whole careers, are wrecked

By any too egregious breach of trust
    Between two basic items in the shrewd
Shakespearean's credo. These advise: adjust

To changing times but don't let that exclude
    Such readings altogether from the fold
Of civilized consensus among clued-

Of critic-types who've figured just how bold
    To be, or not to be.
                Not in the least
Your way, that canny ruse to put on hold

The scope for speculation that increased
    Apace through theory's liberating zest
And so make sure their boundary-pushing ceased

At just the point where commonsense deemed best
    To rein it in. We didn't know, back then,
How soon enough you'd stand out from the rest

As scourge of all like-thinkers, even when
    They thought like you. So, Terry, if I quote
"We shall not look upon your like again"

(Predictably, you'd say) as the right note
    To end on, please forgive this weak resort
To citing just the text you always wrote

About so well: the gesture sells you short.

NOTES

1 *Meaning by Hawkes*: alludes to Terence Hawkes's 1992 book *Meaning by Shakespeare*. This is a typically well-turned title conveying that (1) any meanings we may find in the text are supplied courtesy of Shakespeare, although (2) they are in no way fixed by author's intent or "original" sense, since (3) we ourselves—readers and audiences—"mean by" the plays whatever we take to be their purport or significance as judged by (what else?) our present-day cultural lights. These were, to say the least, controversial claims and were defended by Terry with incomparable verve and resource.

2 *J. Dover Wilson*: For a full-dress treatment of the events, chance encounters, scholarly exchanges, and historical-political context, see Terence Hawkes, "Telmah," in *That Shakespeherian Rag: Essays on a Critical Process* (London: Methuen, 1986), 92–119.

3 *to Greg's critique*: The Shakespeare scholar W.W. Greg had published, much to Dover Wilson's consternation, an article questioning the dramatic coherence of "Hamlet." See Hawkes, "Telmah," for the complex of social-political circumstances around Wilson's reading of this article and its life-changing impact on his subsequent career. My poem gives just the bare bones.

4 *unheimlich*: unfamiliar, strange, with echoes of Freud on the uncanny.

5 *that old imperial theme*: Readings of Shakespeare—such as G. Wilson Knight's book of that title—which emphasize the royalist, conservative, or proto-imperialist aspects of the plays rather than the more subversive

or suggestively dissident aspects stressed by recent left-wing critics.

6 *Traversi and the like*: Derek Traversi is a Shakespeare critic of deeply conservative views (defender of Franco's regime) who can be read as deploying a transcendental (mystical-religious) interpretation of Shakespeare's late tragi-comedies in order to disown any political bias while smuggling in all manner of covert ideological baggage.

7 *Graham Hough*: Cambridge-based literary critic who provoked a sharp response from Terry for some less than positive comments in the *London Review of Books* concerning literary theory and, more specifically, the *New Accents* series. Terry's letter rose to an expertly judged rhetorical climax but ended with a bit of (let's say) knockabout demotic phraseology rarely to be found in such contexts.

8 *cultural materialists*: Movement in British literary criticism and theory, active from the early 1980s on, which sought to place texts in their historical-political and sociocultural contexts of production and reception, generally (though not so much in Terry's case) with an emphasis on the former. In some ways a British counterpart to the US New Historicism, albeit less markedly "textualist" in its orientation.

9 *as Leavisites were prone to scoff*: Reference to F.R. Leavis, the Cambridge-based critic who had much to say about Shakespeare's preeminence as an exemplar of "creative-exploratory" language, and who took a strong (some would say dogmatic) line concerning the "great tradition" of English poetry and fiction. He was also known for coming out forcefully against the claims of literary theory in its various, increasingly prominent forms from the US New Criticism down.

10 *a coast / For its Bohemia*: Much-debated geographical error (maybe joke) in *The Winter's Tale*, which has an account of sailors shipwrecked off Bohemia's nonexistent coast.

11 *by Johnson's time*: Dr. Johnson notoriously had little time for Shakespeare's "quibbles"—his puns, ambiguities, multiplied metaphors, etc.—considering them (along with kindred faults in Donne and other metaphysical poets) just signs of an as-yet barbarous or unreformed language. This extreme, even morbid sensitivity to the threat of linguistic misrule went along with Johnson's typically eighteenth-century horror of its (supposed) social-political equivalent in the mid seventeenth-century English Civil War. Terry did much to make readers aware of these larger cultural investments at stake in such (seemingly) specialist literary-critical debates.

12 *take Armstrong/Fortinbras!*: After various *en passant* allusions to jazz Terry brings his "Hamlet" essay to a half-jesting close by advancing this odd

convergence of names as in truth "no coincidence."

13 *your "Twenty Hamlets" point:* One of Terry's best-known lectures of the 1980s; took the TV cigarillo advert as its launch point for running through twenty sketch-interpretations of the play, thus making his point (see note above) about "meaning by Shakespeare" and the open-ended character of reader-response.

14 *Bakhtinian readiness / To thumb your nose:* Reference to Mikhail Bakhtin, the Soviet critic and theorist who wrote extensively about satire, the carnivaleque, and the many-voiced ("polyphonic") character of novelistic discourse.

15 *when presentism bids our better part:* In his later work, Terry took a stronger line on the impossibility (as he saw it) of our ever escaping the interpretative mind-set—the interests, priorities, and ways of reading—imposed by our contemporary cultural milieu. He and I disagreed on this topic of critical presentism and, especially, about its political implications. But his case in its defense was, as always, powerfully and wittily argued with a constant readiness to engage opposing views in a generous and large-minded way. See Terence Hawkes, *Shakespeare in the Present* (London: Routledge, 2002), and Hawkes and Hugh Grady (eds.), *Presentist Shakespeares* (London: Routledge, 2006).

ON THE PLURALITY OF WORLDS

Now, as in the Ideas of God there is an infinite number of possible universes, and as only one of them can be actual, there must be a sufficient reason for the choice of God, which leads Him to decide upon one rather than another.

—*Gottfried Leibniz*, The Monadology *(1714)*

For if comparative perfection were sufficient, then in whatever way God had accomplished his work, since there is an infinitude of possible imperfections, it would always have been good in comparison with the less perfect; but a thing is little praiseworthy when it can be praised only in this way.

—*Leibniz*, Discourse on Metaphysics *(1686)*

All thought must, directly or indirectly, by way of certain characters, relate ultimately to intuitions, and therefore, with us, to sensibility, because in no other way can an object be given to us.

All the interests of my reason, speculative as well as practical, combine in the three following questions: 1. What can I know? 2. What ought I to do? 3. What may I hope?

The light dove, cleaving the air in her free flight, and feeling its resistance, might imagine that its flight would be still easier in empty space.

—*Immanuel Kant*, Critique of Pure Reason *(1781)*

Each thing's itself and not another thing.
    Thus Leibniz, metaphysically secure
In his conviction that the furthest fling
    Of other-world imagining was sure
To vindicate the actual world and bring
    Fresh proof of God's intent. Although by pure
Hypothesis those other worlds might spring
    Forth defect-free, yet we'd be premature

In thinking ours by contrast not the best
    World possible. Nor should it therefore rate
Among those worlds that failed the litmus-test
    Of what God in His goodness would create
And man's God-given reason thus invest
    With such necessity as must negate
All chance events or happenings that rest
    In fortune's fickle hands. It's our innate

Defects of knowledge only, so he thought,
    Not flaws in this our actual world that leave
Our powers of explanation falling short

Or faculties unable to achieve
The sovereign scope by which they might purport
    To justify God's ways to man, perceive
How our confused cross-stitching must distort
    Truth's fabric, and reveal the perfect weave

Of God's design. For otherwise there's no
    Real obstacle to seeing how such sheer
Contingencies—simply the way things go,
    For better or for worse—might reappear
Transfigured in a light that lets them show
    Up minus all the gaps produced by mere
Extent of ignorance. Then what must flow
    From what, once everything stands crystal-clear,

Will prove (however contrary to all
    The text-book principles) that logic's rule
Extends beyond tautologies that fall
    Within the jurisdiction of those school-
Of-Ockham types still laboring in thrall
    To narrow views. It reaches out, like Boole
Much later, into the expanded ball-
    Park of a logic now deployed as tool

And speculative instrument to link
    Up once again with everything that they,
The strict deductivists, would surely think
    Off-limits. Else contingency might stray
Across that formal buffer-zone and shrink
    The space of reason till it leaves no way
For them to shut and seal the growing chink
    In freedom's wall through which Ananke may

Gain entrance. Then she'll soon put on her dress
　　Of science-led necessity and close
That hole again before the Trojans press
　　Dementedly against it in the throes
Of reason stricken by its own success
　　And looking on as myrmidons depose
Scientia in the terminal distress
　　Of every norm that once gave heart to those

Trained up in her defence. Not so for him,
　　Our trans-world voyager, since reason meant
To Leibniz a conjecture that could skim
　　On wings of thought across the full extent
Of modal logic's most inventive whim
　　Or satisfy pure reason's furthest bent
Of speculative thought in quest to limn
　　Not just the means by which to represent

New worlds but how things stand with them aside
　　From all concern with matters more germane
To us as this-world knowers. What applied
　　In those remoter regions must pertain
With equal force beyond the great divide
　　That, after Kant, would constitute the bane
Of our modernity. Thus "woe betide
　　The dupes of metaphysics"—Kant's refrain—

Would cut no ice for one, like Leibniz, whose
　　Whole enterprise relied on jumping clean
Across those gaps the Kantian would refuse
　　To think of crossing once the risk had been
Made plain to all. Thus: he who misconstrues

Pure reason's proper scope since over-keen
To find some application he can use
    And cash idea as concept will then lose

Not just what any valid exercise
    Of reason in its speculative mode
Might hope to yield by way of pure blue-skies
    Reflection but whatever once bestowed
The knowledge-granting gift to recognize
    How all our epistemic gains were owed
To reason's incapacity to prise
    Concepts from intuitions, or explode

The bounds of sense. If any concept void
    Of sensuous intuition must on that
Account be deemed defective, misemployed,
    Or downright empty, then—Kant's tit-for-tat
Symmetric point—the confidence enjoyed
    By Humean empiricists falls flat
Or finds its naïve certitudes destroyed
    Once knocked into the opposite cocked hat

By Kant's remark that intuitions shorn
    Of concepts must infallibly be blind,
Or lacking in whatever might adorn
    Mere sense with all the attributes of mind-
And-world in cognitive accord. He'd scorn
    Such niceties, would Leibniz, since he'd find
Just signs of weakness in those scruples born
    Of epistemic discipline combined

With displaced religiosity and then
    Raised to the height of self-restrictive zeal
By Kant's resolve to place beyond the ken
    Of human knowers all that might reveal
Some occult truth. Best sublimate the yen
    To know what lay beneath the seventh seal,
Whether the voice divine pronounce amen
    Or reason exercise its old appeal

To metaphysical ideas that soared
    Rhapsodically above the solid ground
Of thought's perceptual anchorage, ignored
    The rule he took such trouble to propound,
And so had all its high gyrations floored—
    As Kant's would-be transcendent dove soon found—
By seeking heaven-haunts that might afford
    Fine views but, when push came to shove, were bound

To leave the winged enthusiast bereft
    Of shove to meet its push. If Leibniz stood
High on the list of old-style rationalists left
    Thus high and dry, there's every likelihood
He'd not reject the charge of having effed
    What Kant deemed the ineffable. For should
That charge not carry a much greater heft,
    So he might ask, if put to those who could,

If so inclined, renounce the Kantian vow
    Of epistemic abstinence, respond
To thinking's distant call, and so allow
    Philosophy to venture far beyond
Thought's customary reach yet still kowtow

To rule-enforcers who'd themselves been conned
By some thought-neutering idea of how
　　Such ventures must stay closer to the *monde*

Quotidien. Here concepts always fit
　　Sense-data perfectly and intuitions match
Their concepts with no gap that might admit
　　Some room for change or let the knower catch
A glimpse of possibilities that split
　　Apart from this, our actual world, and hatch
New worlds where those old intuitions sit
　　Conspicuously awry. Then concepts latch

Onto their sensuous content only by
　　A doctrine-wrenching effort that betrays
How much has been repressed of hopes that lie
　　Precisely in that margin where the ways
Of indurated habit come to vie
　　With speculations guaranteed to craze
(Or so Kant thought) the minds of those who try
　　To stretch their thinking round such out-of-phase

Or off-the-wall projections as enticed
　　Leibniz and company beyond the pale
Of sensuous intuitions that sufficed
　　To keep sound concepts safe within the scale
Of human finitude. Soon the *Zeitgeist*
　　Ensures that his idealist followers fail
To take Kant's point and organize a heist
　　Of Leibniz-type ideas for Hegel's tale

Of spirit in its onward-upward climb
      From primitive sense-certainty, through each
Successive stage of consciousness, till time
      Eventually sees fit for mind to reach
Its goal of Knowledge Absolute. If I'm
      At risk here of appearing keen to preach
From that same Kantian rule-book or to prime
      Aspiring space-doves with the truths he'd teach

To curb their soaring souls, that's not the aim
      Or any part of what I started out
To say in limning Kant's attempt to tame
      Leibnizian flights of reason that would flout
His diktat. Yet Kant's rules defined the game
      Only if he alone was fit to tout,
As truth personified, the final claim
      To fix pure reason's bounds beyond all doubt

And so place Leibniz in amongst the crew
      Of dream-seers, prophets, mystagogues, plain fools,
And all those inner-light enthusiasts who
      Took their own consciences to set the rules
Or with each case to legislate anew
      And signal their defiance of the schools
Where conscience always calls for peer-review
      By which to signify that reason pools

Its limited resources and redeems
      Its good repute. Let's take it Kant was well
Wide of the mark in bracketing the dreams
      Of Swedenborg with thinkers who would tell,
Like Leibniz, truths beyond the strict regimes

Of cognitive command or such as fell
Outside our knowledge-remit since the themes
On which those speculators chose to dwell

Might always prove the sort that must transcend
Its limits. Yet, so doing, they'll not yield
One jot of thought-precision or suspend
One rule of logic to which Kant appealed
In order for their thinking to extend
Way out beyond or way off to left field
Of everything we're meant to comprehend
By Kant's idea of knowledge as tight-sealed

Against such threats. They issue from a far
Away yet oddly close-up realm of what
Surpasses understanding like a star
Too many light-years off to fill a slot
In some star-gazer's list of those that are
Worth looking out for while the rest are not
Since they're best viewed—as Stevens' blue guitar
Was heard—by other types whose favorite spot

For viewing lies some distance off the route
Most traveled. That's for Kantian devotees
Of all that comes mind-processed just to suit
The epistemic need of one who sees
What's plainly there to see or renders mute
All sounds except those pre-attuned to please
Their aural temperament. Should they impute
Tone-deafness to performers in strange keys

Called forth by the remotest overtones
     Or reason's wild excess to those who saw
A multiverse beyond the comfort-zones
     Of this-world knowledge, then perhaps the flaw
May lie more with the well-adjusted clones
     Of common-sense cognition than the straw-
Man target of a thinker who disowns
     Allegiance to what Kantians deem a law

Of all well-regulated thought and yet
     Thereby betray that really it's their lack
Of will to think beyond the ground-rules set
     Down in advance. What but their single-track
Thought processes could guarantee they get
     No further than to package, then unpack
Old concepts, terms, and arguments with net
     Result that they're continually sent back

To square one of the rigmarole begun
     When reason first consented to restrict
Its speculative powers, devoutly shun
     The stratosphere, and heed the interdict
On all new versions of the tale once spun
     By those prophetic souls keen to inflict
Their private fantasies on anyone
     Willing to lend an ear. If Leibniz ticked

One box then it's by doing what appeared
     To Kant mad, bad, or dangerous—or just
Plain idiotic—since his thought-path veered
     Far off the beaten track where one could trust
Sense-data to prevent things getting weird.

Thus it claimed access to such truths as must
Hold good for any world where reason steered
　　The questing intellect beyond earth's crust,

Our actual world among them but construed
　　As full of mere contingencies and hence
Just one amongst the branching multitude
　　Of worlds whose past, present or future-tense
Existence no logician could exclude
　　From being real. This not in some loose sense
With scare-quotes or as philosophic food
　　For thought but as entitled to dispense

With proofs empirical and use the case
　　Of mathematics to convince the crowd
Of sceptics that there's room in reason's space,
　　Objectively conceived, for what's allowed
(Like numbers, sets and functions) its own place
　　Among the items rightfully endowed
With a reality whose knowledge-base
　　Can be as apodictically avowed

As any formal axiom or proof
　　Demonstrative. Raise questions if you will
Regarding whether thought should stay aloof
　　From factual truths or circumstances; still
There's no good reason to suppose we'll goof,
　　As Kant believed, if we rely on skill
In speculative thought to lift the roof
　　On earthbound actuality, instill

A sense of worlds elsewhere, and thus promote,
    Along with that, a feeling for what sets
The actual world apart from those that float
    Before our mental eyes when reason lets
Us think or dream them up. Best we devote,
    As Leibniz did, our minds to that which gets
Us out of using "actual" to denote
    "The only world on which to place our bets"

And shows us how the others might be real
    As ours although non-actual while to them,
Those other-world inhabitants, the deal
    Works in reverse. Why, then, should we condemn
A thinker whose one aim was to reveal
    How rich an actuality might stem
From our existing in a world that we'll
    Perhaps, as thinkers, not allow to hem

Our modal speculations or dictate
    The scope of our conceiving yet whose own
Intramundane complexities we'll rate
    More highly once we've seen how all that's known
Of this world might get lost when we translate
    To those for which there's no Rosetta Stone,
No laws of thought or world that commutate
    Except (so Leibniz held) what could be shown

To have the trans-world necessary kind
    Of *a priori* warrant that obtained
For truthful statements formally defined,
    Like those of maths and logic. So what's gained
By actualists through thinking truths assigned

To sundry worlds unknown is best explained
As what serves most distinctly to remind
    Us stay-at-homes with expectations trained

On this-world evidence that worlds elsewhere
    Are, now as always, how we get a fix
On all things actual, and how far they square
    With things in modal logic's bag of tricks.
Then—for those brave enough to go compare—
    The question's what, in the resultant mix
Of world-constituents, might come to bear
    The hopes of those whose world-allegiance sticks

This side of Shangri-La but never yields
    So far to pessimism as to take
The kind of this-world-only line that wields
    Its actualism as a means to make
Hope's countervailing drive desert the fields
    Of open possibility and shake
All confidence in everything that shields
    The hoper from a knowledge that would break

Their world-inventive nerve or strike them dumb
    When faced with actuality's long haul
Of factual hope-defeaters. Lest we come
    Around to such a verdict let's not fall
Back on the sage advice of those who'd drum
    Into our heads the cynic siren-call
Of that long-serving actualist rule-of-thumb
    Which says we're best advised to just play ball

With this-world norms. Then no thought would betray
   The slightest hint of what might yet unfold
As possible beyond what points the way
   To some result reliably foretold
By reason's basic remit to convey
   Its wordly truth as prudently enrolled
On actualism's side and keep at bay
   All thoughts that Ockham's acolytes would scold

As empty metaphysics. Where they drive
   The point too hard, those sticklers for the good
Of thought's self-discipline, is just where I've
   Said we're most prone to miss the sacred wood
In search of common trees, or to deprive
   Our questing souls of everything that could,
More amply viewed, do wonders to revive
   Our sense of such things as are understood

Only by minds at full creative stretch
   Around those possibilia. They gleam
At every thought's periphery and sketch,
   Each one, a world conceived as if in dream
Yet strictly on condition that we fetch
   From reason's store an apt projection-scheme
By which inventive intellect can etch
   The sharpest images with laser-beam

Intensity. Let's anyway concede
   That Leibniz and his kind not only traced
Alternative world-paradigms that freed
   The mind for exploration but embraced
A here-and-now more intimately keyed

To its nearby world-counterparts. When faced
With these infractions of the one-world creed
　　We'll maybe come to think the actual graced,

Not compromised, by modals that conspire
　　With logic to declare ours not the sole
Reality nor such as would require
　　The sorts of zealous boundary-control
Devised to close our minds to that entire
　　Thought-multiverse where reason has a role
Beyond what falls to it as chief supplier
　　Of grounds to think what's there for us the whole

Of what there is. They got him wrong who took
　　Exception (like Voltaire, though let's admit
His error made *Candide* a splendid book)
　　To all the methods Leibniz used to fit
The worst vicissitudes by hook or crook
　　Into a meliorist scheme of things, acquit
The deity of malice, and (what shook
　　His hard-boiled critics) offer us a kit

Of concepts and devices good for use
　　In any new theodicy that sought
To prove God's loving-kindness. He'd deduce,
　　His critics said, by exercise of thought
Alone the perfect, ready-made excuse
　　For all the grief and suffering they'd brought,
That crew of monster deities from Zeus
　　To a God who, as the Church Fathers taught,

Reserved his choicest punishments for those
   Brave dissidents who counted it depraved,
This worship of a psychopath who chose
   To multiply the joys of souls he'd saved
From hellfire by consenting to disclose
   For their delight how those who'd misbehaved
Were broiling down below. Yet should this pose
   A problem God's apologists have slaved

For centuries to solve, still it's that gloss
   On Leibniz that's gone badly off the rails
And not his brave design to think across
   The boundaries drawn up when there prevails
A mind-set such as couldn't give a toss
   For any modal venture that entails
At any rate some temporary loss
   Of bearings. Thus imagination trails

Not clouds of glory from some dream-world past
   Remembrance but a shift of view that tropes
The actual and allows us to contrast
   Its limiting perspective with the hopes
(Though fears as well) that come when we recast
   Conceiving's role from worlds with which it copes
Familiarly to dealing with that vast
   New range that even those who know the ropes—

Experts in modal logic, sci-fi fans,
   Or thought experimenters—may regard
As altogether surplus to their plans
   And purposes. This means a boarding-card
Good for some short-hop flights or day-trips sans

Passport or papers but, it says, debarred
From taking any longer-range or trans-
　　World jaunt to someone else's far back-yard

Which risks the kind of compass-spin that makes
　　A nonsense of our wishing to return,
Like old Odysseus, and relieve the aches
　　Of home-lament in those who've failed to learn
His lesson. Yet perhaps that's what it takes,
　　That same Leibnizian readiness to burn
All bridges leading home, refuse all stakes
　　Except the riskiest, banish all concern

With scheduling our mental flights to touch
　　Down in our actual world, and so—in brief—
Resolve, like him, to kick away the crutch
　　Of common-sense perception or belief
That's oftenest what actualists will clutch
　　Most tightly when the multiverse motif
Looms up on thought's horizon. If it's such
　　A threat to them, a knowledge-wrecking reef

Of unknown possibilia, let's not leap
　　To the same false conclusion that Voltaire
Was quick to put around and thereby keep
　　Enlightened readers safe from this new snare
Laid down, he thought, by those in whom the sleep
　　Of reason bred not monsters but a rare
And, in its way, quite monstrous will to sweep
　　Aside all pains and evils because they're

(Or so the doctrine held) perceived as freak
    And bad occurrences only by dint
Of our restricted knowledge and our weak
    Since human, all-too-human view asquint.
Hence Voltaire's charge: Leibniz was out to seek,
    In his plurality of worlds, a hint
Of that which so transcended our oblique
    And partial knowledge as to lend a glint

Of God's omniscience to the otherwise
    Contingent-seeming congeries of one
Damn thing after another without whys
    Or wherefores. His would be the story run
By clerics through the ages who'd devise
    Some neat new twist of argument to stun
The sceptic or seek out some novel guise
    For old theodicies that came undone

As soon as one reflected on the plain
    Impossibility that any god
Should have all those perfections that pertain
    To Him by definition yet should nod—
Through boredom, inattention, or a pain-
    Approving relish—when the torture-squad
Gets down to work. Inquisitors re-train
    And only a thick creed-protecting wad

Of moral idiocy keeps them cocooned,
    The theologians, in their fixed idea
That it could make no sense if one impugned
    Either God's pure benevolence or sheer
Omnipotence since a God-concept pruned

Of one or other attribute would veer
Too far off course, then finish up marooned
    In heresy and subject to severe

Doctrinal sanctions of the sort that they,
    God's torturers, could best root out. So if
Voltaire and the enlighteners display
    Such animus in their satiric tiff
With Leibniz, let's not be too quick to say
    They're flat wrong to pick up more than a whiff
Of some addition to the dossier
    Of failed theodicies or some new riff

On those repugnant doctrines that contrived
    To get God off the hook and get around
His (let's say) moral flaws by a revived
    And, as it seemed at least, a more profound
Since axiom-based and logically derived
    Account of how things stood. This made it sound
Plain rational to hold that lives deprived
    Of every good might none the less redound

To God's eternal glory all the more
    Decisively by showing how each stroke
Of what must seem misfortune from the store
    Prepared for our bleak lives by some baroque
Revenger counts as something we should score
    Up, if we weren't such simple-minded folk
And prone to take short views, to the rapport
    Between God's purposes and—where they poke

Satiric fun most sharply—all that goes
   To make the sum of human good viewed *sub*
Specie aeternitatis. Just dispose
   Contingent this-world facts around the hub
Of rational necessity that shows
   What's trans-world valid and you'll have the nub
Of his case, as the Voltaire faction chose
   To take it, for aspiring to the club

Of near-angelic intellect. They claimed
   A moral standpoint hugely in advance
Of those poor sufferers at whom were aimed
   Catastrophes they'd put down to mere chance
But which, once their occurrences were tamed
   By reason's higher law, worked to enhance
God's rule as supreme arbiter unblamed
   For all our human woes. These, at first glance,

Might logically be blamed on God alone
   Since His combined perfections left no gap
Or wriggle-room whereby He might disown
   Responsibility and spring the trap
Set by the humanists and others prone
   At every opportunity to cap
Their arguments by picking that old bone
   Anent how those perfections must run slap

Into some version of the paradox
   Or downright contradiction pointed out
By Schopenhauer. His metaphor still mocks
   The God-defenders and ensures the rout
Of all theodicies that tick each box—

Omnipotence, omniscience about
The future, and (the one that really knocks
    A hole in their defences) what they tout

As the benevolence that must belong
    To God's prime attributes—since, if you try
To square them, you'll encounter something wrong
    Or some pair of them logically awry
(Here Schopenhauer again) whichever prong
    Of this or that dilemma may supply
Your hoped-for means of exit from the throng
    Of those left unresolved. Let's not deny,

In view of this, that they possessed at least
    Some warrant for adopting such a note
Of fierce disdain for Leibniz as high priest
    And architect of all that underwrote
The creed of those whose finer feelings ceased
    At just the point where thoughts of God demote
Thoughts of humanity to a decreased,
    Then obsolescent role which (to misquote

Voltaire) lifts all restrictions on the grand
    Inquisitors and thumbscrew-twisters sold
On *credo quia absurdum* who'd expand
    Their repertoire. For they've thrown off the hold
Of reason or the need to understand
    Such elementary truths as might be told,
So long as reason keeps the upper hand,
    By thoughts of how both parties are enrolled,

Victim and persecutor, in a shared
   Though for the moment skewed predicament
That only those with sympathies impaired
   By some inhuman dogma could prevent
From showing how they might at last be spared
   Yet more such grief if only they'd assent
To reason's view of them as deeply snared
   In a warped actuality. This lent

To all their partial outlooks the same hue
   Of darkness, paranoia, or the blind
Insensate rage of those whose one-world view
   Of things, as they half-guessed, had so confined
Their mental universe that all they knew
   Of other worlds was what they were inclined
By trained predisposition to imbue
   With every bad propensity assigned

To virtue's other by (who else?) those fit
   For its upholding in (what else?) that sole
Truth-territory where virtue's friends acquit
   Themselves with every honour and extol
The virtues that most readily admit
   Themselves alone to the exclusive role
Of truth's true arbiters. For here's the bit
   They miss out, those who emphasise the toll

Of unacknowledged suffering that craves
   No alms for our remembrance when it's set
Against Leibniz's worldview, one that staves
   Off all such pointless tendencies to fret,
Like Johnson reading Shakespeare, when the knaves

Win out and fix things so the virtuous get
    It in the neck, no guardian angel saves
        Them as they fall, or twists of fortune let

The best go to the wall. Yet we'll be wide
    Of the Leibnizian mark if we allow
The reasoned optimism of a guide
    To other worlds beyond the here-and-now
Of this, where we deictically reside,
    To close our more parochial minds to how
Their counter-truths proliferate beside
    A plain-fact record which they may endow

Not with a rankling sense of what we might,
    If luckier, more gifted, more adept,
Or better off have done as if by right
    But what contingency has so far kept,
For us, unactualised. Let's think, despite
    All that may disincline us to accept
The Pangloss view, that maybe with a slight
    Yet crucial tweak his seemingly inept

Since twittering or bright-side take on things
    Could yet turn out—when suitably expressed
In God-free modal form—as that which brings
    No such smug doctrine that would make the test
Of rationality its running rings
    Around whoever doubted this was best
Of all worlds possible despite the slings
    And arrows. These could not be laid to rest

By any sage discounting of the odds
    Against an actual world where every bad
Event or fresh catastrophe shows God's
    To us obscure since long-range plan to add
Some greater good for each new case of sod's
    Law as it seems to those struck by the sad-
To-wretched course of every life that plods
    On doggedly as if to show God had

No part in it. Allow yourself to strip
    The God-talk out, or grant it the degree
Of latitude it might require to tip
    His thinking that way, and perhaps you'll see
How it's those Leibniz-bashers in the grip
    Of this-world prejudice who fail to free
Their thinking from the cynic's wish to nip
    Hope's prospect in the bud by harsh decree

Of a poor metaphysics that abjures
    All thought of possibilities beyond
The narrowest of subsets. This assures
    The Kantians that their concepts correspond
To something really out there, while it cures
    The Leibniz-itch to wave a modal wand
And conjure worlds enough for endless tours
    Of brainsick fabulation. Yet the bond

Thus zealously enforced between what fits
    Our this-world concept-schemes and what pertains
To sensuous apprehension then admits
    No slightest space for thought to break the chains
Of a mind-forged necessity that pits

Brute fact against potential and campaigns
In actualism's cause to call it quits
  With might-have-been so long as thought refrains

From moving on to might-yet-be. It thus
  Forgets Kant's own imperative to think
Things out ourselves, sole means of freeing us
  From mental tutelage, and leaves no chink
Through which thought might acquire the impetus
  To challenge common-sense or break the link
Imposed by mere perceptual habit plus
  Fixed notions. Else we might be on the brink

Of some big upset to the status quo
  In all things pertinent to how we cope
With Kant's three questions, viz: What can we know?
  What can we thinkers reasonably hope?
And then, transcending both, what might bestow
  Best claim to moral goodness when we grope
Our way toward it along paths that go
  The highest route lest reason should elope

With sensuous inclination. This would cause,
  As Kant conceives it, such a major breach
In that whole complex edifice of laws
  He'd set in place that it would offer each
Of us some special plea or get-out clause
  Framed so as to ensure they don't impeach
Our errant will but give themselves some pause
  For thought. Then we'd have ample time to reach

A working compromise with what the strict
    Demand of conscience otherwise would deem
Rightfully subject to its interdict
    As instinct-led, hence lacking the esteem
Due moral agents who'd entirely kicked
    Such variants of the hedonist's old theme
And so, on Kant's ascetic reckoning, licked
    Themselves into good shape. But should this seem
Too rigorist, too anxious to inflict
    Its grim *Wirklichkeitsprinzip* on the dream

Of *Lustprinzip* fulfilled, then we should pay
    More heed to just those thinkers, Leibniz first
And foremost, who not only did away
    With that self-inquisition but reversed
The rule by which Kant sought to hold at bay,
    Though vainly, reason's undiminished thirst
For all the variations it might play
    On every long-familiar theme rehearsed

By dwellers in what actualists regard
    As the one world exclusively composed
Of stuff not just dreamed up. For their trump card
    Of common-sense won't make it seem case-closed
If we continue to reflect how hard
    It is, despite the perils Kant exposed
Along pure reason's (by his lights) ill-starred
    Trajectory, to think he diagnosed

Them spot-on so that in all conscience we're
    Best off not venturing past the limits drawn
By wise epistemologists who fear

To tread where metaphysics may yet spawn
Dream-monsters. Yet beyond that same frontier,
   As Kant well knew, while thought-abysses yawn
On every hand, still we can learn to steer
   A course that might just bring us to the dawn

Of an enlightenment not pre-assigned
   Its concepts, values, or ideas of how
The term "enlightenment" should be defined,
   Since—Kant again—its use must disallow
Our falling-back on thoughts of any mind
   That's not our own, or willingness to bow
To any master-thinker of the kind
   Whose influence we'd have to disavow

If we're to honour Kant's injunction: "Dare
   To know," "Think for yourself," "Let no one tell
You what or how to think." Some say that there
   Can be no reading of it where all's well
About a statement that would somehow square
   Its saying that we should no longer dwell
In passive tutelage and—doctrinaire
   As ever—making it his task to spell

This out as an imperative imbued
   With all the moral force deployed to thwart
Our natural inclinations or preclude
   That bunch from jury service in the court
Of reason. That's how justice looks when viewed
   On terms that all too strikingly comport,
As Lacan said, with those to which the lewd
   Or lunatic mass-torturers resort

In Sade's more graphic renderings of the scene
    Where reason's laws are finally enthroned
And execute their verdicts with machine-
    Like force, precision, and a finely-honed
Ignatian knowledge of just which routine
    Of long-drawn suffering or death postponed
Might, in each case, most aptly intervene
    To capture all the impulses disowned

By fragile ego, twist them into vile
    Self-replicators, and ensure they're spliced,
As Sade decreed, tormentor/victim-style
    In pairs whose mere proximity sufficed
To set things off in that most versatile
    Of choreographies. It's just how Kleist
Supposed the power of dance might so beguile
    The viewer that they're finally enticed

By its perfected form into a state
    Of transcendental apathy, while Keats,
That rapt hellenophile, would correlate
    His urn-tale with the way that art depletes
The living energies of those who wait,
    Like his two lovers, till desire that heats
Their youthful blood must suddenly abate,
    Pure form take hold, and the age-old defeats

Of life by art be pictured in the frieze
    That graced his pot. There's the epitome
Of a "cold pastoral" whose devotees,
    We're left to think, may now at last be free
Of sexual craving and the long disease

Of unrequited lust yet cannot be
Admired or envied since the art that frees
  Them is, Keats tells us, also that which we

Urn-fanciers falsely think provides the one
    Escape-route from those sundry ills that vex
Our creature-lives. For then we'll simply run
    To it, like his poor lovers, because sex—
The act itself, not its preamble spun
    Out to infinity—might unperplex
Their act-delaying hang-ups so that none
    Of art's old power remains to charm or hex

His endless chase, her endless flight, the two
  Of them caught momentarily in that
Suspended instant when he can pursue,
  She slip his grasp, and we still marvel at
This wonder-working gift that can undo
  Time's passage till, at last, its concordat
With life deferred becomes the déjà vu
  Of death-in-life and their long lover's spat

Turns lethal. Sex and violence in suspense,
  Unravished still: surely the best of ways
For well-wrought urn or poem to condense
  The lesson to be read in our four K's—
Kant, Kleist, Keats, and (in the most literal sense)
  The parable of Kafka that conveys
How law inscribes the prisoner's offence
  Directly on his flesh and so displays

To maximum effect the law that binds
    Together charge and judgment, sentence and
Its mode of execution. Whence the kinds
    Of penalty meticulously planned
Not only by administrative minds
    In Kafka's tale but—if it were close-scanned
For evidence—by everything that finds
    A lead role on the inner witness-stand

Of his self-prosecuting need to press
    Such charges and unflinchingly exact
Such retribution as reflected less
    Some fitting verdict on some proven fact
Of guilt but more the craving to confess
    Sins without limit, crimes of thought un-backed
By evidence, and a will to transgress
    Whatever laws of conscience might be stacked

Against him by a superego drilled
    In the old penitential exercise
Of Kant's deontic court. Here reason grilled
    Most fiercely anyone it might chastise
For mere benevolence or an unskilled
    (From reason's standpoint) effort to devise
Some ethic based on that which best fulfilled
    The human need for all that might comprise

A life worth living and—here back to Hume,
    Kant's waker-up—worth living only on
Condition that it not so far presume
    As to place all its eggs in some foregone
Or *a priori* basket with no room

For instinct's prompting or for other non–
Rule-governed ways of thought. So those to whom
    Such rules seem all that we can count upon

For guidance in deciding just which course
    Of action to adopt, or how to judge
A tricky case, or which one to endorse
    When two rules clash, will find a moral fudge
In any notion that the surest source
    Of goodness is a willingness to budge
From principles and precepts. These enforce
    A rule too often grounded in some grudge

Against a view of things that would eschew
    Such self-inflicted quandaries and pin
Its social hopes—its moral values too,
    Since (thus construed) all ethics must begin
And end in interests shared—to what will do
    Most social good, so far as lies within
Our power to judge, when subject to review
    By standards shared by us and those akin

To us. This went beyond mere common taste
    In custom, manners, art, and all that goes
To constitute a sphere of value based
    On culture-wide assent to take in those
Humanity-wide interests that replaced,
    For more enlightened types, a gaze that chose
To pass no further than the limits traced
    By its parochial remit to foreclose

More distant views. Yet taking this as far
  As Kant toward the a priori heights
Where reason does its utmost to debar
  All feelings best assigned, by its own lights,
To mankind's lower nature leaves ajar
  The door to Kafka's world where law invites
Us all, men from the country, to co-star
  In a production where the hand that writes

Our part does nothing more than execute
  That perfect choreography that made
Kleist's *Marionettentheater* so suit
  The idea of a moral order played
Out solely through a register of brute
  Legality where no compunction stayed
The lethal hand of justice. Still it's moot,
  So some will say, whether the Kant-brigade

With all their rules and precepts have done more
  Real moral harm than those who took their lead
From Hume and so allowed the close *rapport*
  Of those well-placed as arbiters to plead
Their privilege as keepers of the score
  Who'd naturally incline, through simple need
Of peer-group approbation, to opt for
  Whatever sorts of judgment best agreed

With views upheld by qualified, i.e.,
  Worth-listening-to and reputable guides
To judgment. Then what counts is how to be
  Both things in virtue of (here bona fides
Become more tenuous) the bourgeoisie

And their idea that really what decides
Our judgment in such matters is the pre-
    Established set of values that provides

Good warrant should we be required to make
    Our case. Thus any doubters who resist
The currency of taste or so mistake
    Their proper role as to suppose we've missed
The point, us dull conformists, and should wake
    Up now at their sharp prompting must exist,
Or so it's held, in some place where to shake
    Things up means treating everything as grist

To this or that consensus-grinding mill
    From which appear such alien sorts of stuff
As have no role to play or slot to fill
    In any scheme of things that's close enough
To ours for us to recognize it still,
    Or it to have at any rate a rough
Equivalent in ours that, with some skill
    In concept-navigation, won't rebuff

Our good-willed efforts. Yet that Humean slant
    Toward consensus as the bottom line
In all such matters makes it seem we can't
    Intelligibly hope to redefine,
As Leibniz did, the very terms that grant
    Pure reason its own licence to assign
Truth-values across worlds in ways that Kant,
    And after him the sceptic Wittgenstein,

Would count mere products of a mind unhinged,
    Or else put down to the malign effect
Of language-games that had for too long binged
    On metaphysics. Thus they'd left unchecked
That power of conjuration that infringed
    The boundary-lines Kant set up to protect
Our faculties against all that impinged
    On them from worlds unable to connect

With ours by any mind-route other than
    The speculative one that took so wild
A course and whose world-divagations ran
    So far from home that nothing reconciled
Its devotees, once voyaging began,
    To making sure a logbook was compiled
So that the journey back should go to plan
    Since every outbound world-change had been filed

For homebound reference. I've taken here
    Some likewise lengthy, even (be it said)
Some flighty ways around to show that we're
    Not always or predictably misled
By thought-experiments that leave the sphere
    Of this-world epistemic grasp and head
Out into waters where the buccaneer
    Of counterfactual travel grasps instead

What's gained when thought foregoes the comfort-zone
    Of a priori knowledge or the just
As reassuring world where things are known
    Or held-true simply through a Humean trust
In the deliverances of those who've shown

Good judgment when such matters are discussed.
Theirs are the verdicts other folk then own
　　As principles that all good judges must,

If they're to count as such, find everywhere
　　Borne out by commonsense and the appeal
To (what else?) plain good judgment since to share
　　Consensus views and values is to feel
On that account entitled to declare
　　How surely one's convictions have the seal
Of best authority. They stand foursquare
　　With what a well-run survey would reveal

Of attitudes on every question deemed,
　　By them and by their peer-group, worth the time
It takes for such a sample of esteemed
　　Respondents to ensure their voices chime
Note-perfectly in any discourse themed
　　To suit (the beautiful and the sublime
Old favorites). Should this latter bit have seemed
　　A string of mere tautologies where rhyme

Made up (perhaps) for the conspicuous lack
　　Of argument or content, then you've got
My point: that making truth in judgment track
　　What's held true by the highest-rated lot
Of savants or some other well-placed claque
　　Of focus-groupies makes us apt to trot
Out the same answers with no more to back
　　Them up than a straightforward appeal to what

Best fits the currency of best belief
    And so lets our truth-values circulate
With maximum liquidity the chief
    Concern. Let's say the Kantians overrate
Pure reason's vigil as a watching brief
    And veto-wielding power to legislate
In every case where truth might come to grief
    On error's shoal. Yet, if we compensate

By swinging right across to take a view
    Of truth as nothing more than lets us gain
Or share the sorts of approbation due
    To those who'd let like-mindedness constrain
Their judgment, or the wish to think on cue
    Whatever some new *Zeitgeist* might maintain,
Then we shall bid *epistêmê* make do
    With *doxa*, knowledge dwell in the domain

Of falsehood, and the claim of truth retreat
    From view. Then we might think the only means
To head off reason's ultimate defeat
    Is to fall back on all the stock routines
That thought adopts when judgment takes back seat
    And its fine art no longer intervenes
To help ensure that reason's standards meet
    Those others set by a behind-the-scenes

Gift for imagining (and here let's pause
    To think once more of Leibniz) how the whole
Of this our actual world and all its laws
    That Kant decreed our concepts should patrol
With utmost diligence might yet show flaws

In just that operation. Its chief role,
Let's then suppose, is to be that which draws
　　A boundary to exact the heaviest toll

Within its power to levy on the likes
　　Of him, our space-time traveller, whose jaunts
Of reason-scripted fantasy or hikes
　　Throughout a modal pluriverse that haunts
Our actual world are sensed as alien strikes
　　By homeguard zealots. Hence the usual taunts
Of those who'd dig such world-protective dikes
　　Of mundane sense against a view that flaunts

Its multiplicity of worlds to bring
　　More vividly to mind how premature
Is any thought that sutures any thing
　　To those known attributes that would secure
Its this-world status safe from any fling
　　Of trans-world voyaging. For it's by pure
Conjecture that new worlds contrive to spring
　　The mind-forged traps that otherwise ensure

We won't risk cutting loose the apron-string
　　Of common-sense by some unscheduled tour
Of *terra incognita* where we'll cling
　　Less tightly to those limits we endure,
Truth is, because they draw the conscience-sting
　　Of knowing how closed world-views may inure
Us finally to hope's unraveling
　　As more worlds vanish from its quadrature.

BEACH SCENE: MÉDUSÉ

Beach scene, good colour snap, you in (I guess)
Your mid-late twenties, head back, curly hair
Like now, full-face to camera, your dress-
Code enigmatic: necklace, sort you'd wear

For parties, skimpy briefs, a slight 'don't mess
With me' look in your eyes, tanned top half bare,
Breasts small and perfect, body language less
A come-on or a keep-off than a dare

To boyfriend, husband maybe: 'sexy, yes,
And necklace quite a turn-on, but take care,
Don't blow your chances - no hope of success
If that bold glance becomes a lengthy stare,

If lust turns dull with craving to possess,
Or this, my self-arousal, fails to scare
You off the very thought that I might bless
Your wish. Plath said it: I eat men like air.

★ ★ ★ ★ ★

That photo: my first sight of it, so not
Quite up to taking all that stuff on board
As if I'd been the guy who took the shot
And there you were, alchemically restored.

Then it would mark some still-familiar spot
Of memory that, with luck, might yet afford
Us both – joint players in that well-made plot –
A leading role. But as it is I'm floored,

Just hunting back for any handy slot
To place it with the other fragments shored
Against the sense of timelines gone to pot
With that one raunchy snap. If someone scored

Back then it wasn't me; if you looked hot,
Or up for it, my share of the reward
Was to have her (you) teach me how I'd got
To live with the idea that some new hoard

Of snapshots might turn up and bring to view
Time-slices of you framed for me by way
Of others' fantasies.

★ ★ ★ ★ ★

Truth is, what threw
Me most was how your image seemed to say

Much the same things to me: 'be careful, you,
My voyeur-lover; there's a price to pay
For ogling this, your extra-special *coup*
De foudre, though you've come late in the day

To gawp at it. No doubt there've been a few
Who gawped, and likely felt the thing convey
Such scary messages, yet still came through
Each time to all appearances OK

And keen for more. Still, best not live to rue
Your back-projected thoughts of me or play
The knowing analyst who takes his cue
From just those details that, he thinks, betray

My one desire: to offer you the clue
By whose unravelling you might allay
Your doubts and fears. No chance: you'll join the crew
Of carved-up suitors, end as easy prey

For curly-haired Medusa, or just do
What that lot did – the guys who figured they
Had me all figured – and so misconstrue
The signs that your desires are led astray

At my least whim. Woe to the ogler who
Doubts this or thinks of my *déshabillé*
In that old snap as just a trick to woo
The male gaze with my pleasing disarray

And tousled curls, as if to prove this shrew
Well tamed. It's not his wishes I'll obey,
Nor yours, nor anybody's in the queue
Of my ex-fanciers who find they may

Have bitten off far more than they can chew
By taking that old beach-scene to display
Past intimacy. What they get in lieu
Of me's an image that begins to fray

Around the edges once the déjà vu
Effect takes hold and memory's *dossier*

D'érotiques comes up with nothing new
To tweak their nerve. So, if you hit the hay

With me and have no secret wish to screw
Some 2-D revenant from *temps passé*,
Then let this living flesh of mine subdue
Your scopic drive and end her overstay.'

www.ingramcontent.com/pod-product-compliance
Lightning Source LLC
Chambersburg PA
CBHW071555110726
47908CB00007B/2105